SENIOR LIVING MARKETING MASTERY

SENIOR LIVING MARKETING MASTERY

How to Fill Every Bed in Your Facility

RONALD OSBORNE

Founder of Senior Living Mastery & Assisted Living Near Mom

Multiple Award-Winning Expert & Published Author

Senior Living Marketing Mastery: How to Fill Every Bed in Your Facility

Copyright © 2026 Ronald Osborne. All rights reserved.

Published by Senior Living Mastery & Ronald Osborne
Fort Lauderdale, Florida
seniorlivingmastery.com

No part of this publication may be reproduced, distributed, or transmitted in any form or by any means without prior written permission of the publisher.

For permission requests, contact: seniorlivingmastery.com

Paperback ISBN: 978-1-7645151-2-2
Ebook ISBN: 978-1-7645151-3-9

First Edition

Printed in the United States of America

DEDICATION

To my loving and amazing wife, thank you for all of your support and all of your love.

To my wonderful son, just keep being awesome.

And to God, for His guidance, His kindness, and His blessings.

Thank you!

Our Marketing Comes With Guarantees

seniorlivingmastery.com/book-a-call

If you are a senior living facility and you want help and advice, our work always comes with a guarantee. That means even if you do not end up working with us, we still guarantee you walk away with valuable and actionable advice. Book a free call today.

CONTENTS

Introduction: Why This Book Exists

Chapter 1: The Senior Living Marketing Landscape

Chapter 2: Understanding The Real Buyer

Chapter 3: Your Website Is Your First Interview

Chapter 4: SEO That Actually Fills Beds

Chapter 5: Google Business Profile Domination

Chapter 6: Content Marketing And Topical Authority

Chapter 7: Link Building And Off-Page Authority

Chapter 8: Paid Advertising That Generates Tours

Chapter 9: Lead Follow-Up That Fills Beds

Chapter 10: Reputation Management And Reviews

Chapter 11: Referral Networks Everyone Ignores

Chapter 12: Converting Tours And Your 90-Day Action Plan

Chapter 13: AI And The Future Of Senior Living Marketing

Conclusion: The Facilities That Win

About The Author

Resources

Appendix: Worksheets, Checklists, and Quick Reference Guides

Notes

Introduction: Why This Book Exists

I did not write this book because I needed another credential. I wrote it because I got tired of watching good facility owners lose money to bad marketing advice.

Let me tell you who I am and why that matters.

My name is Ronald Osborne. I am a former Australian Army veteran who came to the United States and built a telecommunications company called TWECS from zero to $5.7 million in revenue with over 30 employees.

I know what it takes to build a real business from nothing. I have sat in the chair you are sitting in right now. Stressed about payroll, worried about occupancy, wondering why the phone stopped ringing.

After I sold that company, I moved into digital marketing. I built an agency that consistently ranked against some of the largest competitors in the country.

Then I found the senior living space.

Not because someone told me it was a good niche. I found it because I saw an industry full of hardworking operators who were getting destroyed by generic marketing agencies that did not understand the first thing about how families actually choose a facility.

Today I run Senior Living Mastery out of Fort Lauderdale, Florida. We are the only marketing agency in the country built exclusively for assisted living, senior living, and independent living facilities.

We do not work with roofers. We do not work with dentists. We do not take on plumbers or lawyers or chiropractors. We work with facility owners like you. That is it.

The Data Advantage Nobody Else Has

I also own and operate Assisted Living Near Mom. It is a national senior living directory with over 7,000 facilities listed and thousands of monthly visitors.

That directory gives my team and me something that no other marketing agency in this space has. Real data.

We see exactly what families are searching for when they look for assisted living. We see which facilities they click on and which ones they ignore. We see what pages they spend time on and what questions they ask before they ever pick up the phone.

Every single day, that data feeds directly into the strategies we build for our clients.

Generic agencies do not have this. They are taking frameworks they use for HVAC companies and car dealerships and trying to shoehorn them into your industry. That does not work.

The senior living buyer is completely different from any other consumer. The emotional weight of the decision, the family dynamics, the urgency, the trust required to get someone to move their mother into your care. It is unlike anything else in marketing.

We do not guess. We have the actual data. And that data is baked into every chapter of this book.

Proof That This Works

I want to tell you about Sunny Hills Assisted Living in Florida. When we started working with Danny, the President of Sunny Hills, the Sebring location was in serious trouble.

Occupancy was so low that there were genuine conversations about shutting the doors. The writing was on the wall unless something changed.

We rebuilt the marketing from the ground up. We fixed the website. We fixed the reputation. We fixed the follow-up systems. We built out every channel covered in this book.

Sunny Hills now consistently runs above 90% occupancy at both locations. The business has done so well that they are now looking to purchase their third location.

We have worked together for close to five years now. That is not a one-off win. That is sustained, compounding growth built on the systems in this book.

> **BOOK A CALL**
>
> If you have bought this book, we will help you. We offer free 30-minute consultation calls and we guarantee you walk away with actionable information. Even if we never work together, you will leave that call with real, useful advice.
>
> Visit seniorlivingmastery.com/book-a-call

What You Will Get From This Book

This book is structured around 12 chapters. Each one covers a critical piece of the senior living marketing puzzle. Every chapter is based on real strategies we use with real clients. Nothing is theoretical.

You will learn exactly who your real buyer is and why most facilities are marketing to the wrong person.

You will learn what your website needs to look like to actually convert visitors into phone calls.

You will learn how to dominate your local Google search results so families find you instead of your competitors.

You will learn how to run paid ads that generate tours, not just clicks. And you will learn how to build a follow-up system that stops you from bleeding expensive leads.

You will learn how to fix your online reputation, because nothing else works if your reviews are bad.

And you will get a 90-day roadmap that tells you exactly what to do on Monday morning.

Throughout this book, I reference free templates, checklists, and tools that we have built specifically for senior living facilities. You can download all of them at seniorlivingmastery.com/senior-living-marketing-plan. They are free. Use them.

I also reference our YouTube channel frequently. We cover everything about marketing and AI in the senior living space. If you want step-by-step video walkthroughs of anything in this book, visit youtube.com/@SeniorLivingMastery.

Why We Are Different

Let me be upfront about something. This book is packed with useful, actionable information. But I also want you to know that Senior Living Mastery exists to help you implement all of it.

We only work with senior living facilities. Every dollar we spend on research, every tool we build, every strategy we develop is specifically for your industry.

We own Assisted Living Near Mom. No other agency has access to the real family search behavior data that we see every single day from over 7,000 listed facilities.

We work with a guarantee. Most agencies will not put their money where their mouth is. We do. We build guarantees into our agreements because we know the system works.

We offer market exclusivity. If we work with a facility in your city, we will not take on your competitor down the road. Your market is your market.

We are all-encompassing. SEO, paid ads, reputation management, website design, lead nurturing, referral strategy. We handle everything so you do not have to juggle five different vendors who do not talk to each other.

And I literally wrote the book on senior living marketing. You are holding it.

> **FREE RESOURCE**
> Download all templates, checklists, and tools mentioned in
> this book at seniorlivingmastery.com/senior-living-marketing-plan. They are free.

The Cost Of Every Empty Bed

One more thing before we get into it.

Every empty bed in your facility is costing you roughly $68,000 per year in lost revenue. That is not a scare tactic. That is math.

If you have five empty beds, that is $340,000 walking out the door every year.

The strategies in this book are designed to stop that bleeding. Some of them cost nothing. Some require a budget. All of them have been tested and proven.

This book is not a collection of vague marketing tips. It is a playbook. Every chapter has specific actions you can take this week.

I am not going to sugarcoat things or tell you what you want to hear. If your website is bad, I will tell you. If your reviews are killing your business, I will tell you that too.

You did not buy this book for pleasantries. You bought it because you need beds filled. So that is exactly what we are going to do.

Let us get to work.

Chapter 1: The Senior Living Marketing Landscape

The United States assisted living market is worth over $94.2 billion. There are more than 30,000 facilities across the country.

Ten thousand Americans turn 65 every single day. Demand is at an all-time high.

And most facilities are still losing money because of marketing mistakes that would take them a week to fix.

I know because I have seen it firsthand. Through Senior Living Mastery and our Assisted Living Near Mom directory of over 7,000 facilities, I can see the patterns.

I can see which facilities convert visitors into tours and which ones get ignored. And what I see, over and over again, is that most facilities are making the same five or six mistakes.

> **KEY STAT: 4.3 million searches happen every month in the** United States for senior living related terms. If your facility is not showing up in those search results, you are invisible to the families who need you most.

The Six Marketing Mistakes Costing You Residents

I have reviewed hundreds of assisted living facility websites, Google profiles, and marketing campaigns. The same mistakes show up everywhere.

There is a good chance your facility is making at least three of them right now. Let me walk you through each one.

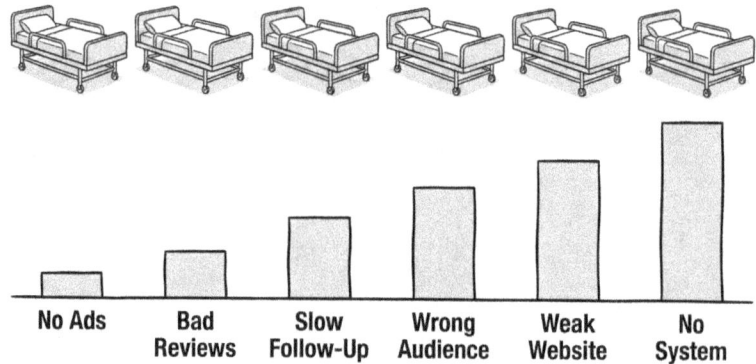

Figure 1.1: The Six Marketing Mistakes Costing You Residents

Mistake 1: No Paid Advertising

Everyone used to rely on organic marketing and word of mouth. Those days are over.

When a family types assisted living plus your city into Google, the first thing they see is paid ads. If you are not there, your competitors are taking those leads before a family ever scrolls down to your listing.

I pull up Google results every single day for different cities across the country. The facilities running smart ad campaigns with proper extensions and call buttons are dominating the top of the page.

The ones relying purely on organic? They are buried. Buried means invisible.

Let me give you a real example. I pulled up assisted living in Fort Lauderdale recently. The top three results were all paid ads. Well-structured ads with site link extensions, call buttons, and multiple click targets.

These facilities were working with smart agencies or they had someone in-house who knew what they were doing. The ad copy was clean. The landing pages were specific to the search.

Below those ads sat the Map Pack. And below the Map Pack, the organic results. A facility relying solely on organic traffic was sitting in position seven or eight.

How many families scroll that far? Almost none. The vast majority of clicks happen in the top three positions. If you are not there, you are not getting those calls.

Google Ads for senior living is genuinely affordable compared to other industries. Cost per click in most areas runs between $3 and $5. Compare that to legal keywords at $25 per click.

You are getting a bargain and most facility owners do not realize it. I break down the full paid advertising strategy in Chapter 8.

Mistake 2: Bad Online Reputation

This is the single biggest issue I see in this industry. It ties into every other marketing channel you operate.

Let me be blunt about this.

If you have a 3.9-star rating on Google with 10 reviews, you are burning money on every other marketing activity you run. Full stop.

You could have the best website in the country. You could have the best ad campaigns and the best SEO strategy.

But if a family pulls you up on Google and sees a poor rating, they are gone. They click back and call your competitor.

Here is why this matters more in senior living than any other industry.

A homeowner might take a chance on a roofer with a 3.9 rating if the price is right. They figure the city would not have licensed him if he was dangerous, and insurance covers mistakes.

But when it comes to placing their mother or father in a facility? No one takes that risk. The scrutiny on reputation in this space is enormous.

> **KEY STAT:** 78% of families trust online reviews as much as personal recommendations when choosing a senior living

> facility. Your star rating is not a vanity metric. It is your first impression.

I have had facility owners contact me when it was already too late. They spent hundreds of thousands of dollars on marketing over two or three years. Their review profile was so damaged that nothing moved the needle.

The writing was on the wall. I had to be honest and tell them to save their money. The venture was over.

I see facilities running ads when they have not even addressed their reputation. Why would you pay to drive traffic to a Google profile that scares families away?

Fix your reputation before you spend a single dollar on anything else. Chapter 10 shows you exactly how.

Mistake 3: An Outdated Or Broken Website

Your website is the first interview a family has with your facility. And most assisted living websites are failing that interview badly.

I review websites constantly. The problems are always the same.

No phone number above the fold. No clear call to action. Stock photos instead of real facility images.

Tiny text that is unreadable on mobile. No pricing information anywhere. No testimonials or reviews on the homepage.

Remember who is visiting your website. It is typically a daughter, aged 45 to 65, who is stressed and searching late at night on her phone.

If she lands on your website and cannot immediately figure out what you offer, how to contact you, and whether you are trustworthy, she clicks back and calls your competitor instead.

I pulled up a facility recently that had been around for over a decade. They had some traffic coming to their site. Decent number of monthly visitors.

But the website was old. The layout was outdated. No phone number above the fold. No clear call to action. When I switched to mobile view, the text was tiny and unresponsive. The contact page was buried three clicks deep.

Meanwhile, their competitor down the road had a clean, modern site with a phone number at the top, a book a tour button in the header, real photos, and reviews embedded on the homepage.

Guess who was getting the tours? The competitor did not have a better facility. They had a better website.

I have seen facilities increase their tour bookings by 50% to 100% just by redesigning their website with proper call to actions and real photos. Chapter 3 covers this in full detail.

Mistake 4: Bleeding Leads

The average cost per lead in the senior living space is around $431. That is what it costs to get one family to raise their hand and say they are interested.

That number is insane. And most facilities are letting those expensive leads die on the vine.

Seventy-eight percent of families go with the first facility that responds. Not the best. Not the cheapest. The first one to pick up the phone.

A five-minute response converts at 100 times the rate of a 30-minute response. Let that sink in.

And the average facility takes 12 hours or more to respond to a web inquiry. Some never call back at all.

I have worked with facilities where we come in and ask about their follow-up process. They tell me they send one email. Maybe a text. That is it.

Meanwhile, they have $431 leads sitting in their inbox collecting dust while the facility down the road called back in three minutes and booked the tour.

When you work with us, the first thing we fix is the follow-up system. Before we touch the website, before we launch ads, before we do anything else.

Because generating leads is pointless if nobody is calling them back. Chapter 9 covers the exact follow-up system we build for every client.

Mistake 5: Targeting The Wrong Audience

Most facilities think they are marketing to the person who will move into the facility. That is wrong.

Your buyer is almost never the resident. Your buyer is the adult daughter, aged 45 to 65, who is searching on behalf of her parent.

She is the one on Google at 11pm. She is the one comparing facilities. She is the one who will pick up the phone and schedule a tour.

If your website says enjoy your golden years in comfort and style, you are talking to the wrong person. That messaging does not resonate with a stressed 52-year-old daughter who is scared about her mother's safety.

It gets worse when facilities run ads. If you are targeting everyone over 65, you are burning your budget on people who are not the decision makers.

Another thing that trips people up. A lot of facilities lump assisted living and memory care into the same marketing campaign. That is a mistake.

Families know that memory care is more expensive than standard assisted living. If a daughter is searching for assisted living and your ads keep showing memory care messaging, she is going to assume your facility is out of her price range. Even if it is not.

You need separate campaigns for each care type. Separate keywords. Separate landing pages. Separate messaging.

The family searching for memory care is in a different emotional state and has different questions than the family searching for assisted living. Treat them differently. Speak to them differently.

And do not mix luxury and affordable in the same campaign. Those two words do not belong together. If you are a luxury facility, market as luxury. If you are affordable, own it. If you are in the middle, stay in the middle.

The facilities that get this right see dramatically lower costs per lead and higher conversion rates. Chapter 2 breaks this down completely.

Mistake 6: No Marketing System

The biggest mistake of all is not having a system. Most facilities are doing marketing in bits and pieces.

Maybe they tried Facebook ads for two months and gave up. Maybe they paid a generic agency that did not understand the industry. Maybe they are relying entirely on referrals from A Place for Mom at $5,000 to $7,000 per placement.

None of that is a system.

A system means every piece of your marketing works together. Your website feeds your SEO. Your SEO feeds your Google Business Profile. Your ads drive traffic to landing pages built to convert.

Your follow-up system catches every lead. Your reputation management makes every other channel more effective. And the data from every channel feeds back into the system so you can see what works and what does not.

It is like going to the gym without a plan. You show up, you do some random exercises, and you wonder why nothing changes. A system gives you structure, accountability, and measurable results.

That is what we build at Senior Living Mastery. And that is what this book will teach you to build for yourself.

> **KEY STAT:** Each empty bed in your facility costs approximately $68,000 per year in lost revenue. Three empty beds? That is $204,000 walking out the door annually.

The Real Cost Of Doing Nothing

Let me put some numbers on the table.

If your facility has 40 beds and you are running at 80% occupancy, that means 8 beds are sitting empty. At an average monthly rate of roughly $5,600 per resident, those 8 empty beds are costing you about $537,600 per year.

Even filling just two of those beds through better marketing would add over $134,000 in annual revenue.

One extra move-in per month at an average stay of 22 months is over $120,000 in lifetime revenue. That one resident covers your entire quarterly marketing spend in the first month.

The math is not complicated. The question is whether you are going to do something about it or keep watching that revenue walk out the door.

What The Top Performers Do Differently

Through our work with dozens of facilities and the data we see from Assisted Living Near Mom, we know exactly what separates the facilities that stay above 90% occupancy from the ones that struggle.

The top performers have a fully optimized Google Business Profile with 50 or more real photos and consistent weekly posts.

They have a website that puts the phone number and a clear call to action above the fold on every page. No exceptions.

They respond to every inquiry within five minutes. Not five hours. Five minutes.

They have a review generation system that produces new Google reviews every single week. Not once a quarter. Every week.

They run targeted Google Ads and Facebook Ads with proper tracking so the algorithms learn who to target.

And they have a follow-up system with 15 to 30 touchpoints over 90 days that keeps them in front of every family until a decision is made.

That might sound like a lot. It is. But every piece of it is covered in the chapters that follow.

And if at any point you look at this and think you do not have the time or expertise to do it yourself, that is exactly what we are here for.

> **WATCH THE VIDEO**
>
> Full video walkthrough of the senior living marketing landscape on our YouTube channel. Search for Senior Living Mastery on YouTube.

Chapter 2: Understanding The Real Buyer

If your website says enjoy your golden years in comfort and style, you need to hear this.

The person reading your website is not the person who is going to live in your facility. It is their daughter.

She is 52. She is stressed. She is sitting in her kitchen at 9pm trying to figure out what to do about her mother.

That is your customer. If you do not understand that, nothing else in marketing matters.

I know this because I see the data every single day. Through Assisted Living Near Mom, I can see exactly what families are searching for, what language they use, what questions they ask, and what makes them click on one facility over another.

The insights we get from this data alone are why we are the leading experts in senior living marketing. I wrote the book on this. Literally.

When we figured this out for Sunny Hills, it changed everything. Their marketing started connecting with the right person, saying the right things at the right time.

They went from a facility that was talking about shutting the Sebring location to a business that is now looking at purchasing their third location. The secret was not a magic ad campaign. It was understanding who the real buyer is and building every piece of marketing around that person.

The Real Buyer Profile

Let me paint a picture of who your actual customer is. Everything I am going to teach you depends on you understanding this person.

Your customer is typically a woman. She is anywhere between 45 and 65 years old.

She has her own family, her own career, her own life. Now she has been thrust into this role of deciding where her parent is going to live. She did not plan for this.

She might have been thinking about it vaguely. But then something happened.

A fall. A diagnosis. A wandering incident. A call from a neighbor saying they found her dad confused in the driveway.

That is usually the trigger event that sets everything in motion.

Figure 2.1: The Real Buyer Profile

The Emotional Profile

Understanding demographics is only half of it. You need to understand the emotional state of the person you are trying to reach.

When a daughter starts searching for assisted living, she is not calm and rational. She is in crisis mode. Something happened, and now she has 20 browser tabs open and a knot in her stomach.

The primary emotion is guilt. She promised herself she would never put her mother in a home. And now she is touring one.

She feels like she should be able to take care of her parent herself. But she cannot. She is working full time. Her husband works full time. She has her own kids at home.

There is a lot of guilt and shame involved in these decisions. That is just the reality.

Secondary emotions include feeling overwhelmed, scared of making the wrong choice, and confused about the process. Most families have never done this before.

They do not know the difference between assisted living and memory care. They do not understand pricing structures. They do not know what questions to ask on a tour.

Her biggest fear is simple. What if they do not actually care? What if it is just a business to them?

What she needs to hear from you is equally simple. Your mom will be safe. You are making the right decision. We treat her like family.

If your marketing communicates those three things, you are ahead of 90% of your competitors.

> **KEY STAT: 67% of assisted living residents are women. 53%** are over the age of 85. But the person doing the searching is almost always under 65. The daughter is the decision maker. She is the buyer.

The Four Stages Of The Family Journey

At Senior Living Mastery, we have mapped out the four stages families go through before a move-in happens. Each stage requires different messaging and different actions from you.

Stage 1: The Trigger Event

Something just happened. A fall, a hospital stay, a diagnosis. The family is in panic mode.

They are emotional and searching late at night. Through Assisted Living Near Mom, we consistently see that the highest volume of searches and contact form submissions happens in the evening. Not during business hours. Not in the morning.

That is a critical insight. If your Google Business Profile shows you close at 5pm, you are hurting your visibility at the exact moment families are most actively searching.

At this stage, families are typing things like signs parent needs assisted living and what do you do when a parent cannot live alone.

They are at the very beginning. If you have content on your website that answers these questions, you are the first facility they encounter. And being first matters more than anything.

Stage 2: Research And Compare

Now they are looking at options. They are comparing three to five facilities. They are reading reviews. They are visiting websites. They are looking at pricing.

At this stage, your reviews, your pricing transparency, your virtual tour, and your comparison content are doing the heavy lifting.

If your Google rating is 4.7 with 120 reviews and your competitor has a 3.9 with 12 reviews, you are winning this stage without spending a dollar on ads.

They are also searching for things like assisted living cost in your state, facility name comparisons, and tour information.

The beauty of our space is that as long as you are in the top three being compared, you are going to get solid leads. Now it is just about closing the deal.

Stage 3: Contact And Tour

They have narrowed it down to two or three options. Now comes the most critical moment.

Seventy-eight percent of families go with the facility that responds first. Not the best. The first.

Sixty percent of tours come from inbound phone calls. A five-minute response converts at 100 times the rate of a 30-minute response.

For smaller facilities that do not have a dedicated person fielding calls, we set up AI systems to handle those initial inquiries. Speed wins every time.

I do not care how nice your building is. If the facility down the street picks up the phone first, they get the tour.

Stage 4: Decision And Move-In

The family is leaning toward you but still needs final reassurance. This stage typically takes 70 to 100 days from first contact.

You will need 15 to 30 touchpoints before they make the final decision. Emails. Text messages. Phone calls. A second tour with a sibling. A testimonial from a current family.

That is why your follow-up system is so critical. Without it, you lose families at the finish line to competitors who simply stayed in touch.

I cover the exact system in Chapter 9.

What Most Facilities Say Vs. What Families Want To Hear

There is a massive gap between how most facilities market themselves and what families actually need to hear.

Most facilities say: Enjoy luxury living. The family wants to hear: Your mom will be safe here.

Most facilities say: State-of-the-art amenities. The family wants to hear: This is how much it costs, and here is what is included.

Most facilities say: Caring and professional staff. The family wants to hear: Meet Sarah. She has been here for eight years and the residents love her.

Most facilities say: Schedule a tour today. The family wants to hear: Here is what to expect when you visit, step by step.

Most facilities say: Award-winning community. The family wants to hear: Read what other families just like you are saying about us.

The left column is corporate marketing. Generic. Stock standard. It says nothing meaningful.

The right column builds trust and speaks directly to the person who is stressed, scared, and making one of the hardest decisions of their life.

See the difference? One talks about you. The other talks about them. Guess which one fills beds.

> **QUICK TIP: Before you publish anything, any ad, any email,** any page, ask yourself: Would this help a stressed-out daughter at 11pm make a decision about her mother's care?
> If the answer is no, rewrite it.

Use your mom, not our patient. Use your father, not our resident. These are the types of words that resonate because you are talking to that stressed individual.

Every single one of the 30,000 facility owners in this country thinks they have the best facility. That is what everyone says. So how do you stand out?

You stand out by speaking directly to the buyer. Not about yourself. About them.

Instead of quality assisted living near you, try: The safest facility in Fort Lauderdale, Florida. Instead of we provide excellent care, try: See what 120 families are saying about us on Google.

That shift in language is small. But the impact on conversions is massive.

Building Your Buyer Persona

We have built a complete buyer persona template that maps out your ideal customer in detail. Demographics, emotional profile, search behavior, decision timeline, objections, and messaging guidelines.

You can download it for free at seniorlivingmastery.com/senior-living-marketing-plan.

Here is an example of what a completed buyer persona looks like.

Name: Sarah. Age: 52. Female. Lives 25 minutes from the facility. Works downtown. Household income $75,000 to $120,000. Married. Two teenagers at home. Sandwich generation.

Daughter and primary caregiver to her 78-year-old mother who has early signs of dementia.

Trigger event: Mom fell at home. Neighbor found her. ER visit. Doctor said she cannot live alone anymore.

Primary emotion: Guilt. Secondary emotions: Overwhelmed. Scared of making the wrong choice. Confused by the options.

Biggest fear: What if they do not actually care? What if it is just a business to them?

What she needs to hear: Your mom will be safe. You are making the right decision. We treat her like family.

Where she searches: Google first. Then Caring.com, A Place for Mom, Assisted Living Near Mom, Facebook groups, Reddit.

Decision timeline: Urgent. 30 to 45 days. Mom cannot go back home.

Facilities she is comparing: Three to five.

Deal breakers: Bad smells, unfriendly staff, hidden pricing, no transparency.

Deal makers: Staff remember her mother's name. Transparent pricing. Happy residents. Clean facility.

Why does this matter? Because this persona directly impacts your ad targeting on Facebook. It impacts the messaging on your website. It impacts the keywords you target in SEO and the scripts your team uses on the phone.

When you know exactly who you are talking to, every marketing decision becomes clearer. Your website copy practically writes itself. Your ad targeting gets sharper. Your content strategy has a purpose.

> **FREE RESOURCE**
>
> Download the Buyer Persona Template at seniorlivingmastery.com/senior-living-marketing-plan. Includes the example above plus a blank template for your facility.

Common Objections And What They Really Mean

When families hesitate, they say things that sound like rejection. But they are almost never actual rejection. They are fear.

When a family says I need to think about it, what they really mean is: I am scared and I need reassurance.

When they say it is too expensive, what they really mean is: I do not understand what is included or how I am supposed to pay for this.

When they say mom does not want to move, what they really mean is: I have not had the conversation yet, and I am dreading it.

When they say we are still looking at other places, what they really mean is: Nobody has made me confident enough to commit.

Understanding the real meaning behind these objections changes how your admissions team handles every single phone call and tour.

Here is a quick example. A family calls and says we need to think about it. Your untrained receptionist says okay, no problem, let me know. The family never calls back.

Your trained admissions coordinator hears the same words and knows it means the daughter is scared. So instead she says: I completely understand. This is a big decision and there is no pressure. Can I ask what specifically is on your mind?

Most of the time, they are worried about one thing. Cost, care quality, or their parent's reaction.

Once you identify the real concern, you can address it directly. And suddenly that we need to think about it turns into: Actually, can we schedule a second visit for my brother to see it too?

That is the difference between losing a lead and filling a bed. I cover objection handling in much more detail in Chapter 12.

> **BOOK A CALL**
>
> If you need help building your buyer persona or understanding who is actually searching for your facility, book a free call.
>
> seniorlivingmastery.com/book-a-call

Chapter 3: Your Website Is Your First Interview

Your website is either your best salesperson or your worst enemy. It works 24 hours a day, seven days a week, and it never calls in sick.

It is the first thing a family sees before they ever pick up the phone.

Having reviewed thousands of assisted living websites throughout my career at Senior Living Mastery and through our Assisted Living Near Mom directory, I can tell you that most of them are actively driving families away.

That is not an exaggeration. When you have a directory of 7,000 facilities and you can see the data on which websites actually convert visitors into inquiries and which ones do not, patterns jump out immediately.

There are specific things that top-performing facilities do on their websites that the bottom performers do not. Most of those things are not complicated. They are not expensive. They are just not being done.

The Fold Line: Your Most Valuable Real Estate

The fold is the invisible line on your website. It is the point where a visitor has to scroll down to see more content.

Everything above that line is the most important real estate on your entire website.

When a family lands on your site, you have about three seconds to convince them to stay. If they cannot immediately see what you do, how to contact you, and why they should trust you, they are gone.

Three seconds. That is it.

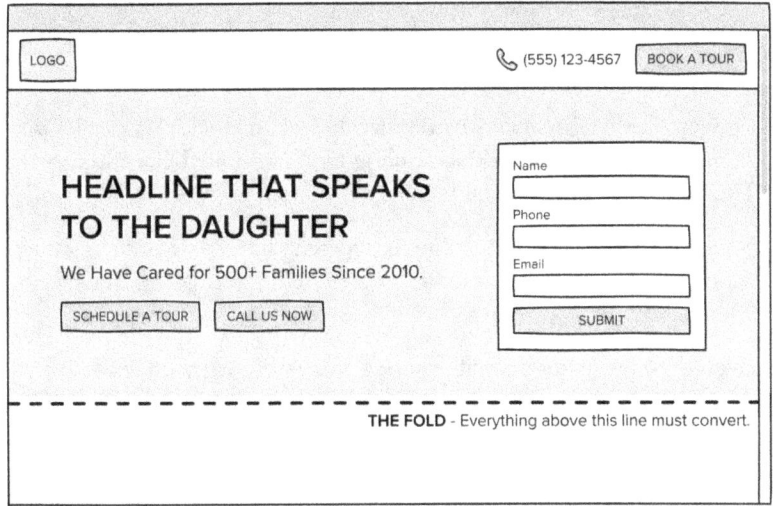

Figure 3.1: The Perfect Assisted Living Website Header

Here is what must be above the fold on every page of your senior living website.

Your phone number. Visible. Clickable on mobile. Not hidden in a hamburger menu. Not tucked into the footer. Right there at the top where anyone can see it and tap it.

A clear call to action. Schedule a tour. Call us now. Book a visit. Whatever language you use, make it obvious and make it easy.

A headline that speaks to the daughter, not the resident. Not enjoy your golden years. Something like: A compassionate home for your loved one in Fort Lauderdale. Trusted by 500 families.

And real photos of your facility. Not stock images. I cannot stress this enough.

Why Stock Photos Are Killing Your Conversions

If you are using stock photos of smiling models who have never set foot in your building, you are starting the relationship with a lie.

Families will see your actual facility on the tour. If what they see does not match the photos on your website, you have already failed to meet their expectations.

And failed expectations are exactly what generate negative reviews.

I reviewed a facility recently that had beautiful stock photos all over their website. Professional models smiling in what looked like a luxury resort. The problem? Their actual facility was a cozy 15-bed home.

Nice, clean, well-run. But it looked nothing like those photos. What happens when a family tours that facility after seeing the website? Disappointment.

Even if your facility is small, show it honestly. A small facility with 10 beds that shows real photos of clean rooms, happy residents, and engaged staff will outperform a large facility hiding behind stock images every single time.

Cameras are good nowadays. Take some photos. Adjust the brightness if needed. If you want them polished, put them on Fiverr and pay a photographer $20 to clean them up. That is better than stock. Every time.

> **QUICK TIP: Optimize for mobile first. Our data from Assisted Living Near Mom shows that 65% to 70% of senior living searches happen on mobile devices. If your site is hard to use on a phone, you are losing the majority of your leads.**

What I See Wrong On Most Websites

Let me walk you through what I see when I review real assisted living websites. I do this constantly and the same problems come up over and over.

I pull up Google, type in assisted living plus a city, and start opening websites. The first thing I look at is above the fold. What am I being told?

On most sites, the answer is nothing useful. A stock image. A vague slogan. No phone number. No call to action. No reason to stay.

Then I check mobile. I switch to a mobile view and the problems get worse. Text too small to read. Buttons too small to tap. Chat widgets that block the entire screen.

Remember who is visiting your website. The daughter. She is on her phone. She is stressed. It is late at night. If your website does not work perfectly on a mobile device, you have already lost her.

Another massive problem I see is the chatbot trap. A lot of facilities use chatbot pop-ups on their websites. Be very careful with these.

They do not always work across all browsers. A lot of ad blockers disable them. And the boomer demographic, which is who we are dealing with, often does not engage with chatbots.

You should never rely on a chatbot as your primary call to action. Your phone number and your contact form need to be right there, visible, no pop-up required.

That said, if you link a chatbot to an AI system, it can be powerful. Someone jumps on your site at 10pm with a question about pricing. The AI chatbot answers immediately. That person books a tour.

But that is a supplement, not a replacement for a proper call to action.

The Sunny Hills Example

When Sunny Hills came on board with us, their website was one of the first things we revamped.

We fixed the basics. Phone number above the fold. Call Homestead. Call Sebring. Right there. Tap to dial.

Real photos. Awards displayed prominently. Services broken out clearly. A YouTube video testimonial from Danny right on the homepage.

The result? Tour bookings increased significantly before we ever touched their ads or SEO. Just from the website revamp.

I have seen this pattern repeat across dozens of clients. Normally around month two, they come back and say Ronnie, we have actually had more tours. We went from 10 tours a month to 15, then 20. What did you do?

The answer is always the same. We just made it easy for families to contact you. That alone is worth a 50% to 100% increase in tours for most facilities.

The 10 Pages Every Senior Living Website Must Have

Based on years of working with facilities and analyzing data from our directory, here are the essential pages your website needs.

1. Homepage

First impressions, hooks, and conversions. This is where your headline, call to action, trust signals, and hero image do the heavy lifting.

Reviews embedded on the homepage. A video walkthrough. Your best testimonial front and center. Danny's case study sits right on the Sunny Hills homepage for exactly this reason.

2. About Us And Our Story

Families want to know who is behind the facility. They want to know your story, your values, and your team.

This page gets more traffic than most owners realize. Through our data, we see that families frequently go straight to the about page and the team page. They want to know who will be caring for their parent.

3. Services

What type of care do you provide? Assisted living only? Memory care? Respite care?

Be specific. If you offer multiple levels of care, break them out. Do not lump everything together. Remember what I said in Chapter 2 about keeping assisted living and memory care separate in your marketing.

4. Pricing

Most facilities are afraid to create this page. That fear is costing them money.

You do not need exact rates. Give ranges. Starting from $3,500 for assisted living. Starting from $5,500 for memory care.

Do not do the $3,000 to $6,000 range. That is too wide. It tells them nothing. Go from $3,500 to $4,500 for assisted living and $5,500 to $7,500 for memory care. That is useful.

A pricing page also filters out families who are not the right fit. That saves you time on leads that were never going to convert. Do not feel bad about that. It happens to us too.

5. Virtual Tour And Gallery

A YouTube video walkthrough is ideal. Just walk through the facility with your phone. Show the common areas, the rooms, the outdoor spaces.

If you do not have video, a gallery of real photos is the minimum. But video converts better because families feel like they have already visited before they pick up the phone.

6. Testimonials And Reviews

Social proof is everything in this industry. Embed your Google reviews. Feature video testimonials.

Get your phone out. Walk up to a resident and say: Susan, you have been living here for three years now. What do you think of the facility?

That 30-second video of Susan saying everyone calls me by my first name and I have friends here is worth more than any stock photo or marketing slogan you will ever create.

Screenshot reviews from Assisted Living Near Mom and other directories. Put them on your website. The more sources of positive feedback a family sees, the more confident they feel about calling.

7. Blog And Resources

This is your content hub. Every blog post you publish is another chance to show up in Google.

You can also use blog content in your follow-up emails. Family had a tour but has not committed yet? Send them your blog post about what to expect in the first month at an assisted living facility. That is valuable content that keeps you in their mind.

I cover content strategy in full detail in Chapter 6.

8. FAQ Page

Address common questions before families even ask. What is the move-in process? Can my parent bring their pet? What if care needs increase?

Every question you answer here is one less barrier between the family and that phone call. Your FAQ page also helps with SEO because these are the exact questions people type into Google.

9. Contact And Schedule A Tour

I recommend two separate pages. A general contact page and a dedicated schedule a tour page.

Some families are ready to book right now. Give them a direct path. Others want to ask a question first. Let them do that too. Do not force everyone through the same funnel.

10. What To Expect And Move-In Guide

Walk families through what happens from first contact to move-in day. This reduces anxiety and builds trust.

The more transparent you are about the process, the more comfortable they feel taking the next step.

The Tech Stack Behind A Converting Website

WordPress is the platform we build on, and for good reason. About 60% of the internet runs on WordPress. It is flexible, it integrates with almost everything, and it is excellent for SEO.

If your website is built on Wix, Squarespace, or GoDaddy, I am going to be honest with you. Those platforms are limited. They are fine for a personal blog. But for a facility that needs to rank in Google, integrate with a CRM, run call tracking, and handle lead forms, WordPress is the way to go.

Here are the systems we integrate with every client website.

CRM integration. We replace the contact form on your website with our own system. Leads go straight into an automated follow-up sequence. Text messages and emails, all personalized, firing out within minutes.

Call tracking. Absolute must. You need to know which marketing channels are generating phone calls. Was it the Google ad? The organic listing? The Facebook campaign? Call tracking tells you exactly where your money is working.

Tour booking tools. Something like Calendly that lets families schedule visits without picking up the phone. Some families prefer to book online, especially late at night when your office is closed.

Review widgets. Free tools that pull in your Google reviews automatically and display them on your website.

Analytics. Google Analytics at minimum. We personally prefer tools that show detailed site behavior, where people go, how they arrived, which pages converted, which ones did not.

Quick Wins You Can Do This Week

If you do nothing else after reading this chapter, do these things. They are free and they will make an immediate difference.

Add your phone number to every page of your website with a click-to-call function on mobile. Go look at Sunny Hills on a phone right now. Call Homestead. Call Sebring. Tap and dial. That is what you need.

Replace any stock photos with real images of your facility. Your phone camera is good enough. Take the photos, upload them. Better than stock. Always.

Make sure your website has an SSL certificate. If your site shows a security warning, you are losing everyone. No family is clicking through that.

Put your content on actual pages, not inside downloadable PDFs. Your pricing, services, and information need to be on the website where Google can index it and families can read it without hoops.

Do not try to hide your pricing behind an email capture form. I know it feels smart, but it is sneaky. Your competitors are going to find out your pricing anyway. Remember who you are trying to talk to. Be upfront.

Remove autoplay media. If someone lands on your website and music starts blasting, they are gone. Make a big play button like YouTube. People will play it if they want to.

Update your copyright year. I see websites showing 2019. Do not be that facility.

Add schema markup. It is search engine and AI language that tells Google exactly what your website is about, what services you offer, where you are located, and how to contact you. It gives you a boost with SEO and it helps AI tools find and reference your facility.

These changes take a few hours. If your website is getting any traffic at all, you will see more inquiries within the first month.

> **WATCH THE VIDEO**
>
> Full video walkthrough of what makes a converting senior living website on our YouTube channel. Real examples, real teardowns. Search for Senior Living Mastery on YouTube.

Chapter 4: SEO That Actually Fills Beds

Right now, there are families in your area searching Google for assisted living. And they are finding your competitors instead of you.

Every single day that happens, that is an empty bed that could have been filled.

Search engine optimization is the process of getting your website and your Google Business Profile to rank at the top of Google. It is not magic. It is not a mystery. It is a methodical process.

When done correctly, it puts your facility in front of families at the exact moment they are looking for you.

I have been doing SEO for many years. I built my own agency to compete against some of the largest companies in the country using these exact principles. And in the senior living space specifically, SEO is one of the most cost-effective tools available.

Why SEO Matters For Senior Living

Seventy-three percent of families start their assisted living search with a generic Google search. Not a specific facility name. They type assisted living near me or assisted living in Fort Lauderdale.

Only about 15% of people already know a specific facility name when they start searching. That means the vast majority of your potential residents are up for grabs.

The question is whether they find you or your competitor.

The Search-to-Move-In Funnel

Figure 4.1: The Search-to-Move-In Funnel

At the top of the funnel, 4.3 million searches happen nationwide every month. Those searches hit Google, where families see three things: paid ads at the top, the Map Pack in the middle, and organic results below.

SEO gets you into the Map Pack and the organic results. Both of those are free traffic. You do not pay per click. Once you rank, the leads keep coming.

Your website then converts that visitor into an inquiry. Your follow-up system closes the deal. Every piece of this funnel matters. But it all starts with showing up in the search results.

> **KEY STAT:** Facilities ranking in the top 3 positions on Google capture the vast majority of clicks. If you are on page 2 or beyond, you are essentially invisible.

Before You Spend A Dollar: Check The Numbers

Before you invest any time or money in SEO, you need to assess whether the juice is worth the squeeze. I always stress this to facility owners.

They might watch one or two YouTube videos and think SEO is the right move. That is not always the case.

I have an MBA specializing in finance. I turn everything into numbers. And the single most common mistake I see facility owners make with SEO is investing without checking the ROI first.

We built a free SEO Forecasting and ROI Calculator that you can download at seniorlivingmastery.com/senior-living-marketing-plan. It walks you through evaluating your keywords, estimating traffic and revenue, and determining whether SEO makes financial sense for your specific market.

Here is the short version. You need to know three things.

One: How many people are searching for your main keyword each month? For most mid-sized metros, assisted living plus your city gets 500 to 2,000 searches per month.

Two: How strong is the competition? If the top results are national directories like A Place for Mom or Caring.com, do not try to outrank them organically. They have hundreds of employees. But you can absolutely compete in the Map Pack where local facilities have the advantage.

Three: What is the lifetime value of a single move-in? At an average stay of 22 months and a monthly rate of $5,600, that is over $120,000. Even if SEO takes six months to produce results, one additional move-in covers the entire investment many times over.

If the numbers are green, go for it. If they are red, put your money somewhere else. It is that simple.

The SERP Volatility Analyzer

We also built a SERP Volatility Analyzer. This tool tests how strong or weak the competition is for your target keywords before you spend anything.

Here is why this matters. You might look at the search results and think it looks easy. But if you run the volatility report and it comes back as hard for positions one through three, you could waste thousands of dollars trying to rank there on your own.

If it shows moderate or opportunity, you might be able to do this yourself by following everything in this book and our YouTube videos.

If it shows hard, you are going to need help. That is where an agency like us comes in with the experience and resources to compete at that level.

Either way, check the data first. Twenty minutes of research can save you thousands of dollars in wasted spend.

> **FREE RESOURCE**
>
> Download the SEO Strategy Checklist including the ROI Forecaster and SERP Volatility Analyzer at seniorlivingmastery.com/senior-living-marketing-plan. All free.

Keyword Research For Senior Living

Keyword research is the foundation of everything in SEO. You need to know what families are actually typing into Google.

Start with Google itself. Type your main keyword into the search bar, like assisted living plus your city, and look at the autocomplete suggestions.

Those suggestions are real searches that real people are making. Low income assisted living. Luxury assisted living. Best assisted living. Each of those is a potential page on your website.

Here is the key insight. Do not limit yourself to one keyword.

If you only rank for assisted living plus your city at 1,000 searches per month, that is good. But if you also rank for best assisted living plus your city at 880 searches, and ALF plus your city at 500, and memory care plus your city at 600, now you are looking at nearly 3,000 potential searches per month.

That is how smart facilities dominate their local market. They do not chase one keyword. They build a web of related terms that all funnel traffic to their website.

Scroll down to the People Also Ask section. Every related question Google shows is a content opportunity. How much does assisted living cost in Florida? Who is eligible? What is the difference between assisted living and memory care?

Each of those questions can become a blog post that ranks in Google. I cover this in detail in Chapter 6.

Competitor Analysis: Let Google Tell You What Works

You do not need to reinvent the wheel. Google is literally telling you what works by showing you who ranks at the top. Your job is to figure out what those competitors are doing and do it better.

For each of your top competitors, you want to know their domain authority, how many keywords they rank for, how many backlinks they have, and how many referring domains point to their site.

These numbers tell you exactly what you are up against.

I pulled up a facility in Tampa recently that was sitting on page four of Google for their main keyword. They had an authority score of 21, 206 keywords, and about 115 referring domains.

On paper, those numbers are not terrible. They should have been ranking higher. So what was going on?

When I dug into the data, the website was not aligned with what Google wanted to see. The content was thin. There was no topical depth. They had a few pages about their services but nothing that demonstrated authority on assisted living in Tampa.

Meanwhile, their competitors in positions one through three had 300-plus keywords, strong backlink profiles, and content that covered every angle a family might search for.

The fix was not complicated. It was methodical. Map out the keyword gaps. Create content to fill them. Build some targeted backlinks. Optimize what is already there. Within a few months, the needle started moving.

That is the beauty of SEO for senior living. The competition at the local level is not as fierce as people think. Most of your competitors are not doing any of this. So a facility that follows a structured approach can break into the top positions faster than you would expect.

The Map Pack Vs. Organic Rankings

There is an important distinction you need to understand. The Map Pack and organic rankings are two different games.

The Map Pack is the three-pack of local businesses that shows up with a map when someone searches. It is powered primarily by your Google Business Profile, your reviews, and your proximity to the searcher.

Organic rankings are the regular website listings below the Map Pack. These are powered by your website content, your backlinks, and your on-page SEO.

For most local facilities, the Map Pack is where you should focus first. Here is why.

National directories like A Place for Mom, Caring.com, and assistedliving.org dominate the organic results. They have massive websites, thousands of backlinks, and hundreds of employees. You are not going to outrank them organically for your main keyword.

But in the Map Pack? They cannot compete. The Map Pack rewards local businesses. Your facility, with a strong Google Business Profile, good reviews, and consistent local signals, can absolutely rank in the top three.

I cover Google Business Profile optimization in full detail in Chapter 5. But understand that for most facilities, the Map Pack is where the money is.

On-Page SEO Essentials

On-page SEO is everything you do on your own website to help Google understand what your pages are about.

Your primary keyword needs to be in the page title, the first paragraph, and at least one subheading. It also needs to be in the meta title.

Keep your meta title under 60 characters and your meta description under 155 characters.

Content needs to be substantial. At least 1,500 words on main service pages and blog posts. Google rewards depth, but only when it is useful. Do not pad with fluff.

Include your city name naturally throughout the content. If you are in Fort Lauderdale, mention Fort Lauderdale multiple times. This signals to Google that your content is locally relevant.

Use at least five subheadings per page. Short paragraphs. Three to four sentences maximum. Nobody reads walls of text, and Google knows it.

Add real images with descriptive alt text. Your facility photos can rank in Google Image search, which is another traffic source most facilities ignore.

Internal linking is critical. Link your blog posts to your service pages. Link your services to your pricing page. Link everything to your contact page. This structure distributes ranking power across your entire site.

Why SEO Matters Even More Going Forward

AI is changing how people search. ChatGPT, Google's AI Overviews, Perplexity, and other tools are pulling information from websites and presenting it to users in conversational summaries.

If your website has strong, well-structured content, AI tools will reference you. If your website is thin or outdated, you will be invisible to the next generation of search.

I believe we are moving toward a world where traditional browsers become less dominant. People will interact with AI assistants that pull information from across the web and present it in conversation.

When a daughter asks an AI assistant to find the best assisted living facility in Fort Lauderdale, that AI is going to reference the facilities with the strongest online presence. The most content. The best reviews. The most authority.

SEO also ties directly into reputation management. If an AI chatbot summarizes your facility and pulls in negative reviews, that impacts how families see you before they ever visit your website.

The more positive, authoritative content you have online, the better your facility looks across every channel. Including AI.

Investing in SEO today is not just about ranking in Google. It is about building a digital footprint that serves you everywhere families look.

WATCH THE VIDEO

Full video walkthrough of senior living SEO strategy on our YouTube channel. Includes live competitor analysis and keyword research demos. Search for Senior Living Mastery.

BOOK A CALL

If you want us to conduct a full SEO audit of your facility, book a free 30-minute discovery call. We will show you exactly where you stand.

seniorlivingmastery.com/book-a-call

Chapter 5: Google Business Profile Domination

When a family types assisted living near me into Google, they see the Map Pack. Three facilities. Name, rating, review count, phone number.

If you are one of the three, you are getting calls. If you are not, you barely exist.

Through our Assisted Living Near Mom directory of over 7,000 facilities, I can see exactly which Google profiles generate inquiries and which ones collect dust. The patterns are obvious. And most of the fixes take less than a weekend.

Your Google Business Profile is the single most important free marketing asset your facility has. It is more important than your website for local visibility. It is the first thing most families see. And it is where the majority of local searches convert into phone calls.

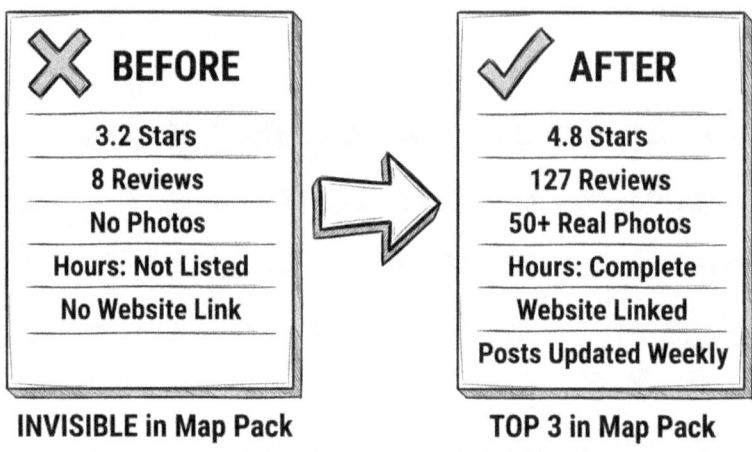

Figure 5.1: Google Business Profile: Good vs. Bad

Claim, Verify, And Take Full Control

You would be surprised how many facility owners have unverified Google profiles. Sometimes Google creates a profile automatically based on directory listings and other online mentions.

Your facility might already have a Google profile that you did not create. Type your facility name into Google right now and find out.

Once you find it, claim it and verify it. This is step one and it is non-negotiable.

Make sure you have admin or owner access. Not manager access. This is critical, especially if you have ever worked with a marketing agency before.

I have had clients come to us after firing their previous agency only to discover that the agency owned their Google Business Profile. The facility owner was listed as a manager and could not make changes without the agency's permission.

That is a nightmare. Do not let it happen to you. You must own your profile.

The NAP Alignment Rule

NAP stands for name, address, and phone number. These three pieces of information must be identical everywhere they appear online. Your Google profile, your website, your directory listings, your social media, everywhere.

Not similar. Identical.

If your Google profile says 1715 NE 4th Avenue and your website says 1715 North East 4th Avenue, that is a mismatch. Google's algorithm sees that as conflicting data.

I reviewed a facility recently where the phone number on Google was different from the phone number on the website. It was a call tracking number that someone had swapped in and forgotten about.

That one mistake was hurting their Map Pack ranking. The profile was sending conflicting signals to Google. Garbage in, garbage out. That is how algorithms work. You feed it clean data, it rewards you. You feed it conflicting data, it punishes you.

Go through your website, your Google profile, your citations, and your directory listings right now. Make sure everything matches exactly. This alone can move the needle.

> **QUICK TIP:** When Google abbreviates directions like NE or NW in your profile, match that on your website. Do not spell out North East on one and use NE on the other. Consistency is everything.

Categories: Get Them Right

Your primary category should be Assisted Living Facility. Check this. You would be surprised how many facilities have the wrong category set.

Some have Nursing Home listed. Some have Rehabilitation Center. Some have categories that have nothing to do with assisted living.

If your primary category is wrong, you are telling Google you are something you are not. Fix it immediately.

Secondary categories matter too. If you offer memory care, add Memory Care as a secondary category. If you also provide nursing home services, add that. But the primary must be Assisted Living Facility.

I cannot overstate how much this matters. I have seen facilities jump multiple positions in the Map Pack just by correcting their primary category. It is that impactful.

Business Hours: Stop Hurting Yourself

This one catches people off guard.

If your Google Business Profile shows operating hours of 9am to 5pm, you are hurting your visibility during the exact hours when families search the most.

Through Assisted Living Near Mom, we consistently see that the highest volume of searches and contact form submissions happen in the evening. Not during business hours. Not in the morning. The evening.

There is also a spike around lunchtime. But the majority of traffic comes after 5pm.

If Google sees that you are closed when a family is searching, it will deprioritize you in favor of a facility that is listed as open. Open 24 hours, 7 days a week is the setting you want.

Your facility does not close. Care is provided around the clock. Someone can always answer the phone. List your hours accordingly.

Photos: The Difference Between 8 And 50

Businesses with photos on their Google profiles get 42% more direction requests and 35% more website clicks. That is not opinion. That is Google's own data.

I pulled up three facilities competing for the same keyword in Tampa recently. One had 8 photos. One had 28. One had 51.

The one with 51 photos was outranking the others in the Map Pack despite having fewer reviews. Interesting, right?

Photos tell Google that your business is active, legitimate, and well-maintained. They also give families a reason to click on your profile instead of your competitor's.

Here is the photo strategy we use with every client.

Exterior photos. Five to ten minimum. Front entrance, signage, parking area, building from multiple angles. Show families what they will see when they pull up.

Interior and common areas. Living rooms, dining areas, activity spaces, kitchens. Real photos, not staged. Show the facility as it actually looks on a normal day.

Resident rooms. At least five examples. Clean, well-lit, and inviting.

Staff interacting with residents. Get consent first, obviously. But these are the most powerful photos you can post. A caregiver sitting with a resident, helping with an activity, sharing a laugh. That is the photo that makes a daughter pick up the phone.

Outdoor spaces. Especially if you are in a warm climate. Gardens, courtyards, patios, walking paths.

Seasonal updates. Christmas decorations. Easter events. Summer activities. Upload new photos every month. Google rewards fresh content. It shows your profile is active and that real activity is happening at your facility.

Your target should be at least 50 photos. If you are under that, start uploading this week.

> **KEY STAT: Businesses with 50+ photos on their Google** Business Profile receive significantly more engagement than those with fewer than 10. Upload real, current photos of your facility every single month.

Google Posts: Worth The Effort?

Google Posts used to be one of the most powerful tools for Map Pack rankings. Back in 2018 through 2023, posting every day could significantly move the needle.

That has changed. Posts still help, but they are not the ranking lever they used to be.

My recommendation is to post at least once a week if you have the time. If you are on a tight budget and need to prioritize, put your time into photos and reviews instead.

When you do post, include a photo with every post. Add a call to action. I recommend the Call Now button over Learn More because phone calls are what fill beds.

Good post ideas include activity and event highlights, staff spotlights, seasonal content, new amenities or services, and community updates.

If a resident's family member visits and has a wonderful experience, that is a post. If your team throws a birthday party for a resident, that is a post. If you just finished renovating the garden, that is a post.

Keep it real. Keep it warm. Keep it consistent.

Reviews: The Number One Ranking Factor

Reviews are the single most powerful factor for Map Pack rankings. More important than photos. More important than posts. More important than categories.

It is not just about the number of reviews. It is also about how the reviews are written.

Reviews that mention your services, your facility name, and your location carry more weight with Google's algorithm. A review that says Great assisted living facility in Fort Lauderdale, the staff here took amazing care of my mother is more valuable than a review that just says Nice place.

Your target should be one new review every single week. That is 52 reviews per year. In two years, you have over 100. That puts you ahead of most competitors in any market.

> **KEY STAT:** 78% of families trust online reviews as much as personal recommendations when choosing a senior living facility. Your review count and rating are your most powerful marketing assets.

How To Generate Reviews Consistently

Create a Google review link from the backend of your Google Business Profile. It takes 30 seconds.

Take that link to a free QR code generator like qrcodegenerator.com. Download the QR code. Print it and place it at the front desk, in common areas, and anywhere families gather.

Train your staff to ask for reviews after positive moments. Family visits. Events. Care milestones. When a family member says something positive about the facility, that is the moment to ask.

Here is the script I teach my clients. Susan, your daughter just told me she is so happy with how her mother has been doing here. It would mean the world to us if you could share that experience in a quick Google review. It takes about one minute. Can I show you the QR code right now?

That is how you get reviews. In the moment. When the emotion is positive and genuine.

Do not automate this. I cannot stress this enough. If you set up an automated review request system that fires off to every family after a tour, you will inevitably send it to someone who was not happy. And that is how you get one-star reviews that destroy your profile.

Manual selection. Every time. Only send the review link to families and visitors who had a genuinely positive experience.

One more thing. Each resident typically has three to ten family members. Each of those family members is a potential reviewer. One resident can generate three to ten reviews over their stay. There is no excuse for not building a strong review profile.

Responding To Every Review

Respond to every single review. Positive and negative. Every one.

For positive reviews, a simple thank you and a personal touch goes a long way. Thank the reviewer by name. Reference something specific if you can.

For negative reviews, remember this. Every negative review exists because you failed to meet someone's expectations. That is the psychology behind it.

The response formula is straightforward. Thank them for the feedback, even if it stings. Acknowledge their specific concern. Take it offline by offering a direct phone number or email. And explain what you are doing to fix the issue.

I have seen one-star reviews turned into five-star reviews using this approach. And here is the surprising thing. A one-star to five-star flip is more common than a one-star to three-star. When you show genuine care and accountability, people respond to that.

If the review is clearly fake or from a competitor, say so publicly. We do not have a record of anyone by this name at our facility. We would love to address your concerns directly. Please call us at this number.

Then report it to Google as spam. If you need help removing fraudulent reviews, that is something we handle for our clients.

Citations: Your Local SEO Foundation

A citation is any online mention of your facility's name, address, and phone number. Think of directory listings.

Assisted Living Near Mom. Caring.com. A Place for Mom. Senior Advisor. Yelp. Bing Places. Apple Maps. Better Business Bureau. Your state's assisted living directory. Yellow Pages. Super Pages.

Each of these citations reinforces to Google that your facility is real, legitimate, and located where you say it is.

The key is consistency. Every single citation must have the exact same NAP information. Same name. Same address format. Same phone number. Any variation weakens the signal.

We built a free citation analysis tool that scans your online presence and identifies inconsistencies. You can find it in the resources at seniorlivingmastery.com/senior-living-marketing-plan.

Get listed on at least 20 to 30 quality directories. Focus on senior living specific directories first, then general local business directories, then industry directories.

The Three Things To Do This Week

If you can only do three things from this chapter, do these.

First, claim and fully complete your Google Business Profile. Every field. Every category. Full description with your services mentioned. Hours set to 24/7.

Second, upload at least 50 photos. Follow the photo strategy I outlined. Exterior, interior, rooms, staff, outdoor spaces, events. Real photos. Not stock.

Third, set up your review generation system. Create the Google link. Generate the QR code. Train your staff on when and how to ask. Set a target of one new review per week.

These three actions alone will move your Map Pack ranking. I guarantee it.

Chapter 6: Content Marketing And Topical Authority

Every day, thousands of families type questions into Google about assisted living. How much does it cost? What are the signs my parent needs care? What is the difference between assisted living and memory care?

Real searches. Real volume. Real families looking for answers.

Most facilities have zero content answering any of these questions. And that means they are invisible to the families asking them.

A facility with 50 blog posts on its website has 50 chances to show up in Google search results. A facility with zero blog posts has zero chances outside of its homepage.

Every blog post is a net you cast into Google. More nets, more fish. It is that simple.

The Five Content Pillars

At Senior Living Mastery, we have developed a content framework built around five pillars. These pillars cover every type of question a family might ask during their search.

Pillar 1: Education

This is the broadest pillar and the most important one to start with.

Topics include what assisted living actually is, the difference between assisted living and memory care versus nursing homes, what to expect in the first month, and how the admission process works.

Education content catches families at the very beginning of their journey. They do not know what assisted living is. They do not understand the differences between care types. Your content answers their first questions, and that positions you as the authority from day one.

Pillar 2: Cost And Financial

This is the number one question families ask. How much does it cost?

Create content around assisted living costs in your specific state and city. Cover topics like whether Medicare covers assisted living, VA Aid and Attendance benefits, long-term care insurance, and how to financially plan for assisted living.

Pricing content does double duty. It attracts traffic from Google and it pre-qualifies families before they ever contact you. If your pricing is transparent, the families who reach out already know what to expect.

Pillar 3: Decision Support

These are the emotional and practical articles that help families take the next step.

Signs your parent needs assisted living. How to talk to your parent about moving. What to look for on a facility tour. Questions to ask before choosing a facility.

This pillar is incredibly powerful because it targets families at the exact moment they are deciding. If your facility is the one helping them navigate this decision, you have already built trust before they ever pick up the phone.

Pillar 4: Local Content

This is your competitive advantage as a local facility.

Best assisted living in Fort Lauderdale. Assisted living options near downtown Miami. Senior care facilities in Broward County.

National directories cannot compete with you on hyperlocal content. They write generic national articles. You write about your specific community, your specific neighborhood, your specific city.

Local content also reinforces your geographic relevance to Google, which directly helps your Map Pack rankings.

Pillar 5: Lifestyle And Trust

This pillar showcases the human side of your facility.

Activities and events at your facility. Resident stories and testimonials. Staff profiles. Day-in-the-life content. Community partnerships.

This content does not always drive huge search traffic. But it is powerful for social media, email follow-ups, and building trust with families who are already considering you.

When a daughter is comparing three facilities and she sees one of them has a blog full of photos and stories about real residents living happily, that tips the scale.

Topic Research: Let Google Tell You What To Write

You do not need to guess what to write about. Google will tell you.

Go to Google and start typing your main keyword. Before you hit enter, look at the autocomplete suggestions. Those are real searches that real families are making in real time.

Type assisted living plus your city and watch the suggestions populate. Fort Lauderdale. Near me. Facilities. Cost. Reviews. Each of those is a content opportunity.

Scroll down to the People Also Ask section on any search results page. Those are the exact questions families are asking. How much does assisted living cost in Florida? Who is eligible? What is the average cost?

Every single one of those questions can become a blog post that ranks in Google and drives traffic to your website.

You can also use Google Keyword Planner for free. Set up a Google Ads account, which costs nothing, and access the Keyword Planner tool to see search volumes and related keywords.

> **QUICK TIP: We built a free AI prompt that generates a full**
> content strategy for your facility. Just fill in your
> facility name, location, services, and unique selling

> points, and it produces titles, outlines, and a content calendar. Download it at seniorlivingmastery.com/senior-living-marketing-plan.

Blog Post Requirements

Every blog post you publish should meet these minimum standards.

At least 1,500 words. That is the threshold where Google starts to take content seriously. Short posts do not rank.

Your primary keyword must appear in the title, the first paragraph, and at least one subheading. It must also be in the meta title.

Mention your city or area name naturally at least two to three times throughout the content. This signals local relevance.

Use at least five subheadings to break up the content. Short paragraphs. Three to four sentences maximum. Nobody reads walls of text, and Google penalizes pages with poor readability.

Include at least one internal link to another page on your website. Link your cost article to your pricing page. Link your what to expect article to your tour booking page. This structure distributes ranking power across your entire site.

Meta title under 60 characters. Meta description under 155 characters. At least one real image with descriptive alt text. No stock photos.

Your facility photos can rank in Google Image search. Families search for images of assisted living facilities all the time. If your blog posts use real photos with proper alt text, that is another traffic source most competitors ignore.

How Many Posts And How Fast

If you are creating 50 blog posts as part of a comprehensive content strategy, space them out over time. Two to three per week gives Google a steady stream of fresh content to index.

If you are starting with 15 posts or fewer, put them all up at the same time. That signals to Google that your website just got a major content upgrade, which can trigger a re-crawl and faster indexing.

Either way, the key is to start. One post per week is 52 posts per year. In one year, you have a content library that most of your competitors will never match.

Link Building: Why It Matters

Content alone is not enough. Google needs to see that other websites trust your content. That trust signal comes from backlinks.

A backlink is a link from someone else's website to yours. When a reputable website links to your facility, Google interprets that as a vote of confidence.

Think of it this way. If I run around in the street shouting that the sky is falling, nobody listens. If someone with authority says the same thing, people pay attention.

Backlinks work the same way. A link from Caring.com or your local Chamber of Commerce or a hospital in your area tells Google that your facility is legitimate, trusted, and relevant.

You do not need thousands of links. Twenty to thirty quality, relevant links from trusted sites in your area can be enough to push past your local competitors.

Where To Build Links

Senior living directories are your first stop. Assisted Living Near Mom, Caring.com, A Place for Mom, Senior Advisor. If you are not listed on these, fix that today. Each listing gives you a link and a citation.

Local directories are next. Your Chamber of Commerce. Local business directories. Better Business Bureau. State assisted living directories. These carry strong local authority signals.

Partner links come from the relationships you already have. The hospitals, physicians, and clinics that refer patients to you. Ask them to link to your website from theirs. Offer to do the same. A mutual link between a local doctor's website and your facility is a powerful trust signal.

Local PR is another opportunity. Pitch your local newspaper about a story. A new facility opening. A community event you hosted. An award you won. Each article that mentions your facility with a link back to your website boosts your authority.

Guest content is writing articles for other websites in your space. A local health blog. A community newsletter. An eldercare information site. You provide valuable content, they provide a link back to your facility.

HARO, which stands for Help a Reporter Out, is a platform where journalists look for sources for their articles. If your facility has a compelling story or expertise to share, you can pitch journalists and earn links from major publications.

That is exactly how I have been featured in Entrepreneur, Forbes, the New York Times, and other major outlets. I pitched my story and my expertise. You can do the same with your facility.

> **KEY STAT: A facility with zero blog posts has zero chances** of showing up in Google for informational queries. Every blog post is another net cast into the search results. More nets, more fish.

Building Topical Authority

Topical authority is the reason Google shows my content when someone searches for senior living marketing. Google has determined that Senior Living Mastery is the authority in this space based on the volume, depth, and consistency of our content.

You can build the same thing for your facility in your local market.

When Google sees that your website has 30 blog posts covering every aspect of assisted living in Fort Lauderdale, from costs to care types to touring guides to family resources, it starts to treat your site as the local authority on assisted living.

That authority compounds. Each new piece of content reinforces the signal. Each backlink strengthens it. Over time, you start ranking for keywords you did not even target because Google trusts your site on the entire topic.

This is the long game. It does not produce results overnight. But once it kicks in, the traffic is consistent, the leads are free, and your competitors cannot catch up without doing the same work.

If you want to build topical authority fast, combine the five content pillars with a consistent publishing schedule and a targeted link building campaign. That is the formula.

FREE RESOURCE

Download the Content and Link Building Strategy Checklist including the AI content prompt at seniorlivingmastery.com/senior-living-marketing-plan. All free.

WATCH THE VIDEO

Full video walkthroughs of content marketing and link building for senior living on our YouTube channel. Search for Senior Living Mastery on YouTube.

BOOK A CALL

If you want us to build out your content strategy and handle link building, book a free 30-minute discovery call. seniorlivingmastery.com/book-a-call

Chapter 7: Link Building And Off-Page Authority

In Chapter 6, I covered the basics of link building and where to start getting links. This chapter goes deeper.

I am going to show you how to evaluate link quality, how to avoid destroying your website with bad links, how to build a targeted outreach campaign, and how to develop the kind of off-page authority that makes Google treat your facility as the trusted source in your area.

Most facility owners think of links as a checkbox. Get listed on a few directories and move on. That approach gets you to the starting line. It does not win the race.

The facilities that consistently rank in the top three positions for their keywords have a deliberate, ongoing link building strategy. They are not just collecting directory listings. They are building relationships, earning mentions, and positioning themselves as the local authority on senior care.

What A Backlink Actually Does

A backlink is a link from someone else's website to yours. When a reputable website links to your facility, Google interprets that as a vote of confidence.

Think of it this way. If I run around in the street with no clothes on saying the sky is falling, nobody listens. If someone with authority and credibility says the same thing, people pay attention.

That is exactly how links work. A link from your local hospital or your county's aging services department tells Google that your facility is legitimate, trusted, and relevant. A link from a spam directory that lists every business on earth tells Google nothing useful.

You do not need thousands of links. Twenty to thirty quality, relevant links from trusted sites in your area can be enough to push past your local competitors. That is a realistic number for any facility to achieve within six to twelve months.

What Makes A Link Valuable

Not all links are created equal. A link from your local hospital's resource page carries far more weight than a link from a random blog with no traffic.

Google evaluates links based on several factors. The authority of the linking website. The relevance of the content surrounding the link. Where the link sits on the page. And whether the link appears natural or paid.

A link from a high-authority, locally relevant website is worth more than a hundred links from low-quality directories.

In the senior living space, the most valuable links come from healthcare organizations, local government resources, community organizations, news outlets in your area, and senior care directories with real traffic.

A link from your county's aging services department, for example, is a strong signal that your facility is a legitimate, trusted resource. A link from a spam directory that lists every business in every category is worth almost nothing.

How To Evaluate A Potential Link Source

Before you spend time pursuing a link, ask three questions.

First, does this website have real traffic and real content? A website with 10 pages and no visitors is not worth your time.

Second, is this website relevant to senior living, healthcare, or your local community? A link from a Fort Lauderdale health blog is far more valuable than a link from a generic national directory.

Third, would this link make sense to a real person? If a human reader would look at the link and think that is a helpful resource, Google will likely feel the same way. If it looks forced or out of place, it probably is.

> **WARNING**

> Do not go online and buy cheap backlinks. This is the fastest way to permanently destroy your website's rankings. Google penalizes sites with unnatural link profiles, and those penalties can be impossible to recover from. Your domain could be finished forever. Be strategic. Be accurate. Quality over quantity, every single time.

Where To Build Links

Senior Living Directories

Your first stop. Assisted Living Near Mom, Caring.com, A Place for Mom, Senior Advisor. If you are not listed on these, fix that today. Each listing gives you a backlink and a citation that reinforces your legitimacy in Google's eyes.

These directories exist specifically for your industry. When Google sees that your facility is listed on the major senior care platforms, it confirms that you are a real assisted living provider offering real services. That signal matters.

Local Directories And Organizations

Your local Chamber of Commerce, Better Business Bureau, state assisted living directories, and city business listings all carry strong local authority signals.

Get listed on every legitimate local directory in your area. If you are in Fort Lauderdale, you should be on Fort Lauderdale's business directory, Broward County's resource pages, and any regional healthcare directories specific to South Florida.

These links do double duty. They boost your authority in Google and they put your facility in front of families who browse those directories directly.

Healthcare Partner Links

You already have relationships with local healthcare providers. Doctors, hospitals, rehabilitation centers, home health agencies. These are your best link building partners.

Approach them with a simple offer. You refer patients to each other. You serve the same community. A resource page on their website that lists trusted local assisted living options is valuable to their patients and their SEO.

Frame it as a partnership, not a favor. Something like: We would love to be included on your senior care resources page. We can also add a link to your practice on our community partners page. That way families have a complete picture of the care options in our area.

Most healthcare providers will say yes because it genuinely serves their patients. And a link from a hospital or medical practice in your city is one of the most powerful signals you can get.

Local Media And PR

Your local newspaper, community blog, and regional news stations are always looking for stories. The senior living industry provides plenty of angles.

A new facility opening. An expansion. A community event you hosted. A staff member who went above and beyond. A partnership with a local hospital. An award your facility received. Each of these is a pitch to your local media.

When the article runs, it includes a link to your facility. That link comes from a high-authority, locally relevant source. Exactly what Google values most.

Press releases work for genuinely newsworthy events, but do not send a press release every month about nothing. Journalists ignore facilities that cry wolf. Save your pitches for real stories.

Guest Content

Writing articles for other websites in your space is one of the most effective link building strategies available.

A local health blog. A community newsletter. An eldercare information site. A regional parenting website that covers sandwich generation topics. You provide valuable content, they provide a link back to your facility.

Here is an example. You write an article titled Five Questions Every Family Should Ask Before Choosing an Assisted Living Facility for a local health website. The article is genuinely useful. At the bottom, it includes your name, your facility, and a link back to your website.

That one article gives you a relevant backlink from a trusted source, positions you as a local expert, and puts your facility in front of families who are actively researching care options. One piece of content, three wins.

HARO And Journalist Outreach

HARO, which stands for Help a Reporter Out, is a platform where journalists look for sources for their articles. You sign up, receive daily emails with journalist queries, and pitch yourself as an expert when a relevant request comes through.

This is exactly how I have been featured in Entrepreneur, Forbes, the New York Times, and other major outlets. I pitched my story and my expertise. You can do the same with your facility.

When a journalist writes about senior care trends, aging in place, or healthcare topics and includes a quote from you with a link to your facility, that is a backlink from a major publication. Those links carry enormous authority.

Not every pitch will land. But the ones that do can transform your link profile overnight.

How Many Links Do You Actually Need

The answer depends on your competition. In the SEO audit from Chapter 4, you analyzed your competitors' backlink profiles. That gives you your target.

If your top three local competitors have 80 to 150 referring domains and you have 12, you know the gap. You do not need to close it overnight. But you need a plan to close it steadily.

A realistic goal for most facilities is two to three new quality links per month. That is achievable through a combination of directory listings, partner outreach, local media, and guest content.

Over the course of a year, that is 24 to 36 new links. Combined with the directory links you build in month one, you could have 50 or more quality backlinks within twelve months. For most local markets, that is enough to compete for the top positions.

The Cost Of Building Links

In the healthcare space, quality links typically cost between $150 and $350 each when you factor in the time for outreach, content creation, and relationship building.

Some links are free. Directory listings, membership organizations, and partner exchanges cost nothing but your time.

If you work with an agency, link building is usually built into the monthly retainer. At Senior Living Mastery, it is part of every campaign we run because without links, the rest of the SEO work cannot reach its full potential.

The key is consistency. A steady stream of two to three new links per month is far more effective than building 20 in one burst and then doing nothing for six months. Google rewards sustained, natural link growth. Spikes followed by silence look artificial.

Protecting Your Link Profile

Bad links can actively hurt your rankings. And in competitive markets, some facility owners engage in what is called negative SEO. They point hundreds of spam links at a competitor's website to trigger a Google penalty.

This is rare, but it happens. If you suddenly see an influx of links from irrelevant or suspicious websites, that is a red flag.

Google provides a tool called the Disavow Tool that allows you to tell Google to ignore specific links pointing to your site. If you discover spam links, you can submit them through Google Search Console and Google will stop counting them against you.

Most facilities will never need to worry about this. But if you are in a competitive metro area, monitoring your backlink profile quarterly is a smart habit. Tools like SEMrush and Ahrefs make this simple.

> **QUICK TIP**
> You do not need thousands of links. 20 to 30 quality, relevant links from trusted sites in your area is enough to push past most local competitors. Focus on healthcare partners, local directories, community organizations, and media. Two to three new links per month is the target.

Chapter 8: Paid Advertising That Generates Tours

Referral agencies charge $5,000 to $7,000 per placement. That is your first month's rent gone for one referral. One.

Communities running their own ads properly have driven cost per move-in to a few hundred dollars. Not thousands. Hundreds.

That is the difference between giving away your revenue and controlling it.

I am going to break down every advertising platform that exists for senior living and tell you exactly which ones are worth your money and which ones will waste it.

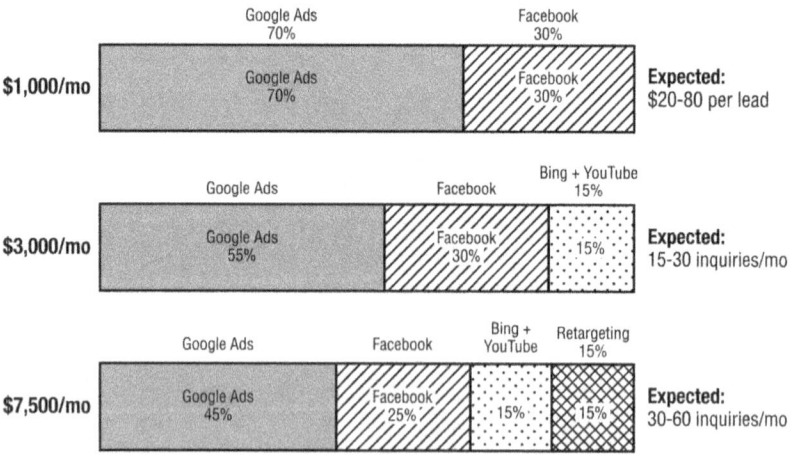

Figure 8.1: The Ad Budget Allocator by Platform and Tier

Google Ads: Your Number One Platform

Google Ads is number one for senior living. Full stop. No debate.

You are reaching families at the exact moment they type assisted living near me into Google. That is intent. They are not browsing. They are not scrolling. They are actively looking for a place for their parent right now.

When I pull up Google for any city, the first three or four results are paid ads. Even before the Map Pack. If you are not there, you are handing those families to your competitors.

Campaign Structure

One campaign per care type. Assisted living gets its own campaign. Memory care gets its own. Respite care gets its own. Do not lump them together. Different services, different keywords, different landing pages.

Inside each campaign, keep your ad groups tightly themed. Three to five keywords per group maximum. Keep them focused.

Target keywords like assisted living plus your city name, assisted living near me, memory care plus city name, and best memory care near your city.

Cost Per Click And Cost Per Lead

The cost per click in most areas runs $3 to $5. Compare that to legal keywords at $25 per click. Senior living is genuinely affordable on Google and most facility owners do not realize it.

Cost per lead on Google runs $20 to $80 in most markets. In competitive metro areas like Miami, Los Angeles, or New York, it can push to $100 or $150.

Even at the expensive end, at $100 per lead with a 10% conversion rate to move-in, your cost per move-in is roughly $1,000. Compare that to $5,000 to $7,000 per placement from a referral agency. The math is not close.

> **KEY STAT: Cost per click on Google for senior living** keywords runs $3 to $5 in most markets. That is a fraction of what legal, dental, and home services pay. You are getting a bargain.

Location Targeting

Suburban markets work best with a 10 to 25 mile radius around your facility. Urban markets need to be tighter, 5 to 15 miles. Rural facilities may need to go as wide as 20 to 50 miles.

Families want their parent close. Your targeting should reflect the realistic driving radius that families are willing to accept.

Ad Scheduling

This is something most people miss. Families do not search for assisted living at 2pm on a Tuesday while they are at work.

Peak search times are Sunday and Saturday evenings between 7pm and 10pm. Monday mornings from 8am to 11am are strong. And there are consistent spikes during lunch hours across the week.

Adjust your ad schedule to increase bids during those peak windows and decrease or pause during low-traffic hours. This stretches your budget and puts your ads in front of families when they are actually searching.

Ad Copy That Converts

Speak to the family, not the facility. Assisted living for your loved ones beats award-winning senior care every single time.

Nobody cares about your awards when they are scared about their parent's safety.

Include call extensions with your local phone number. Add location extensions linked to your Google Business Profile. Use sitelink extensions pointing to your tour page, pricing page, and about page. Give families every reason to click.

Landing Pages: Where Most Facilities Blow It

Most facilities send ad traffic to their homepage. That is a mistake.

Build a dedicated landing page for each care type. The headline must match the search. Phone number visible above the fold. Tour booking form right there. Two to three testimonials at minimum. A pricing range so families know what to expect.

If you are a luxury facility and someone searching for affordable care clicks your ad, a pricing range on the landing page filters them out before they waste your time on a call. If you are affordable, the pricing range attracts the right families and gives them confidence to take the next step.

Facebook And Instagram Ads

Facebook is your number two platform. But it serves a different purpose than Google.

Google catches the family that is actively searching. Facebook catches the adult daughter scrolling at 11pm because her mom just had a fall and she is starting to think about options. She has not Googled anything yet. She is not that far along. But it is on her mind.

That is who you are reaching on Facebook. Top-of-mind awareness for families who are not ready to search yet but will be soon.

> **KEY STAT: 62% of online adults aged 65 and older are on** Facebook. Adult children aged 45 to 65 are Facebook's core demographic. This is where your buyers spend their evenings.

Targeting On Facebook

Age range should be 45 to 65. Never go below 40. The geographic radius should match your facility's realistic service area.

Interest targeting is where Facebook gets powerful. Target caregivers, senior care, sandwich generation, AARP members. You can also target people whose parents are above a certain age, which is incredibly effective for this industry.

Ad Creative

Use real photos of your facility. Not stock. A video walkthrough of 60 to 90 seconds filmed on your phone outperforms any static image.

Emotional headlines work best. Making the right decision for mom should not feel this hard. Your parents deserve more than a waiting list. Speak to the fear, the guilt, the uncertainty that families are feeling.

Video testimonials from residents or family members are the most effective creative you can run. A 30-second clip of a daughter saying the staff here treats my mom like their own family will outperform any graphic design you could produce.

Lead Forms Vs. Landing Pages

Facebook offers in-platform lead forms with lower friction. Families can submit their information without leaving Facebook. These generate higher volume but sometimes lower quality because people fill them out casually while scrolling.

Sending traffic to a dedicated landing page produces fewer but higher quality leads. Families who click through to your website and complete a form there are further along in the decision process.

My recommendation is to run both and compare the results for your specific market.

Retargeting: Facebook's Superpower

Someone visits your website but does not call. Maybe they found you through a Google search or stumbled across your site. Facebook allows you to show ads to that person for up to 30 days.

They see your facility everywhere they scroll. Your photos. Your testimonials. Your name. Over and over.

This is how you stay present during the decision process, which typically takes 70 to 100 days from first contact to move-in. Retargeting keeps your facility at the front of their mind while they compare options.

Facebook Budget And Timing

Do not spend less than $500 per month on Facebook. The sweet spot is around $1,500. Average cost per click is about $2.

Remember that Facebook leads are earlier in the journey than Google leads. They need more nurturing. Your follow-up system, covered in Chapter 9, is critical for converting Facebook leads into tours.

Best times to run Facebook ads are evenings and weekends. Saturday and Sunday are strong performers.

Seasonal note: January and February are peak months for senior living inquiries. Families visit over the holidays, see how their parent is doing, and start searching in the new year. Increase your ad spend during those months.

Platforms That Do Not Work

Let me save you some time and money.

TikTok. Users aged 45 and older grew 120% since 2019. Sounds impressive until you look at the real numbers. Only 14% of people aged 55 to 64 use TikTok compared to 62% on Facebook. It is not ready for senior living ads. Maybe in five years. Not today.

LinkedIn. Fantastic for business-to-business marketing. Not where families search for assisted living. Nobody opens LinkedIn to find a facility for their parent.

X, formerly Twitter. Zero search intent for senior living. Zero visibility for this audience. We test it regularly and have seen nothing positive.

Bing And Microsoft Ads

Do not ignore Bing. It is the default search engine on every Windows computer. The older demographic disproportionately uses it because that is what was there when they first started browsing.

Clicks are cheaper than Google. And here is the best part. You can import your entire Google Ads campaign into Bing in about five minutes. Same keywords, same ads, same structure.

That five minutes of work can generate an extra 10% to 15% of leads at a lower cost per click. It is the easiest win in paid advertising.

YouTube Ads

YouTube is owned by Google, so the targeting capabilities are strong. But you need a solid video to make it work. A walkthrough of your facility or a testimonial from a resident filmed at a reasonable quality.

YouTube works best as a secondary channel. Someone visited your website but did not convert. They are now watching YouTube. Your facility ad plays before their video. They see the building, the staff, a happy resident sharing their experience.

That can be the nudge that brings them back. But get Google and Facebook running properly first. YouTube is the third or fourth addition, not the first.

Budget Allocation By Tier

Here is how I would allocate your ad budget based on what you have available.

Starter budget of $2,000 to $3,000 per month. Put 75% into Google Ads and 25% into Facebook. Google is where the intent is. If you are desperate and need tours quickly, Google is sometimes slow in the first month or two as the algorithms learn your audience. But once it dials in, the leads are consistent.

Growth budget of $3,000 to $5,000 per month. Shift to 60% Google, 25% Facebook, and 15% Bing. Adding Bing at this stage gives you incremental leads at a lower cost.

Scale budget of $5,000 to $10,000 per month. Split it 50% Google, 30% Facebook, 10% Bing, and 10% YouTube. At this level, you have the budget to invest in video production and test YouTube as a retargeting and awareness channel.

A budget of $1,500 to $3,000 per month should generate 15 to 35 leads. Some of our clients at the higher end generate 40 to 60 leads per month.

Tracking: If You Are Not Measuring, Stop Spending

If your facility is not tracking where the money is going and where the leads are coming from, you are wasting every dollar you spend on ads.

Set up Google conversion tracking tags on your website. Install the Facebook pixel. These are non-negotiable.

Tracking is not just for your benefit. It trains the algorithms. Google and Facebook use conversion data to figure out who your ideal lead is. Without that data, they are guessing. With it, they get smarter every day.

I have worked with facilities that spent $5,000 on Facebook over two months and said nothing happened. When I looked at their setup, the Facebook pixel was never installed. The algorithm had zero data to learn from. That is $5,000 thrown away because of a setup step that takes 10 minutes.

Track your leads. Measure cost per lead by platform. Calculate cost per tour and cost per move-in. If the numbers are trending down month over month, your campaigns are working. If they are flat or climbing, something needs to change.

> **FREE RESOURCE**
> Download the Budget Allocator, Lead Tracker, and ROI Calculator at seniorlivingmastery.com/senior-living-marketing-plan. Built specifically for senior living facilities.

> **WATCH THE VIDEO**
> Full video breakdown of senior living PPC strategy on our YouTube channel. Includes live campaign setup and budget allocation examples. Search Senior Living Mastery.

> **BOOK A CALL**
> If you want us to set up and manage your paid advertising,

book a free 30-minute discovery call.
seniorlivingmastery.com/book-a-call

Chapter 9: Lead Follow-Up That Fills Beds

Thirty-nine percent of assisted living leads wait 12 or more hours for a response. Some never get a call back at all.

The average facility I work with has a two to three day response time when we first come on board. Two to three days. In an industry where the data shows that the first facility to respond wins the business nearly every time.

If you have 12 leads sitting in your inbox right now that nobody followed up on, that is roughly $62,000 in annual revenue walking out the door. That is not a scare number. That is math based on average bed rates and conversion data.

Generating leads is only half the equation. If nobody calls them back, you might as well light your marketing budget on fire.

When we came on board with our first major client, the first thing we fixed was not their website. Not their ads. Not their SEO. It was the follow-up system. That single change started filling beds before we touched anything else.

At Senior Living Mastery, what we specialize in is driving lead costs down. The industry average is $431 per lead. Our clients operate well under $100. The difference is not magic. It is follow-up systems that never let a lead go cold.

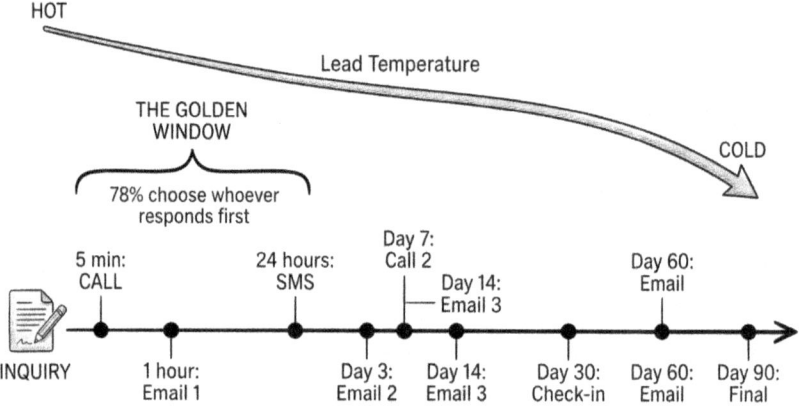

Figure 9.1: The Lead Follow-Up Timeline

The 90-Day Email Nurturing System

I have built a tool that generates a complete 90-day email nurturing system for your facility. It takes about 30 to 45 minutes to set up accurately, and then it runs on autopilot.

Here is how it works.

You fill out a detailed profile document. This is not a basic contact form. It covers your facility's leadership and their background story, your values and philosophy, care types and bed count, licenses and accreditations, your ideal family profile and buyer persona, where your leads come from, real family success stories with detail, testimonials from at least three families, your current offers and incentives, your competitive landscape including what your competitors do well and where they fall short, and your preferences for email tone, length, and sequence duration.

Why does all of that matter? Because you are going to feed this document into an AI tool like Google Gemini or ChatGPT. The AI uses every detail you provide to generate a 20-email sequence that is completely personalized to your facility, your voice, your market, and the families you serve.

The output is not generic marketing fluff. It is hyper-personalized emails that speak directly to the families in your pipeline. The more detail you put in, the better the output.

What The Emails Actually Look Like

Let me give you an example of the immediate response email the system generates.

It opens with something like: Thank you for reaching out. I know that searching for senior care is often overwhelming. You have likely had 20 tabs open on your computer and a knot in your stomach wondering if you are making the right choice. Please take a deep breath. You are doing the right thing by researching.

Then it introduces the Executive Director by name, mentions how long they have been in senior care, and offers a five-minute phone call. Not a sales pitch. A conversation. It includes a direct phone number. It closes with warmth and zero pressure. It even says: We will help you figure this out, even if our facility ends up not being the right fit.

Compare that to what most facilities send. An auto-reply that says: Thank you for your inquiry. Someone will be in touch shortly.

Which one do you think converts? Which one makes a scared daughter feel like she found someone who actually cares?

Using Real Stories In The Sequence

The most powerful emails in the sequence use real family success stories from your facility. Not generic testimonials. Specific, detailed stories that address the exact emotional barriers families face.

Here is an example from one of the sequences we built. The email tells the story of an 84-year-old man named Frank who was living alone and had lost 20 pounds in six months. His three kids were in different states, New York, Atlanta, and Denver, and they were arguing about what to do. One wanted home care. One wanted assisted living. One thought dad was fine.

The facility hosted a virtual tour with all three siblings on Zoom. They agreed to try a two-week respite stay. By day three, Frank was playing cards in the common room. By the end of the two weeks, he told his daughter he liked it there. The food was good and the staff were nice to him. He gained eight pounds in his first month. The siblings stopped fighting.

That email closes with: If your family is struggling to agree on the next steps, let us help you. We can host a family meeting or a virtual tour to get everyone on the same page.

That is a real story addressing a real emotional barrier. It is not selling. It is connecting. And it is why this system works.

> **KEY STAT: Families who tour your facility convert at 35%.**
> Families who do not tour convert at 2%. Everything in your follow-up system should be designed to get families through your front door.

The Follow-Up Cadence

Here is the exact cadence I recommend for the first 90 days after a lead comes in.

Day one. Immediate response within five minutes. Phone call first. Always call first. If no answer, send the personalized email and an SMS immediately after. The SMS should be short and personal. Something like: Hi Sarah, this is Maria from Sunny Oaks. I just sent you an email. I know this process can feel overwhelming. I am here whenever you are ready to talk.

Days two through seven. Daily touchpoints. Alternate between email and SMS. Each message should provide value, not just ask for a tour. Share a success story. Answer a common question. Offer a helpful resource. Address a specific fear.

After the first week, space it out. Twice a week for weeks two and three. Then once a week for the remainder of the 90 days.

By the end of the sequence, you will have made 20 or more touchpoints with that family. Some will convert at email three. Some will convert at email 17. The ones who would have been lost without follow-up are the ones who convert in the back half of the sequence. Those are the beds your competitors never fill.

One thing I want to be clear about. After the first week of daily contact, do not keep hitting them every day. People get frustrated. Space it out, keep the tone helpful, and never sound desperate or pushy. The goal is to stay present without becoming annoying.

SMS: The Secret Weapon

SMS has a significantly higher open rate than email. Most text messages get read within three minutes of being sent.

Use SMS for the high-urgency touchpoints. The initial response. The day-after follow-up. The tour reminder. The post-tour check-in.

Keep the messages short, warm, and personal. Never send bulk marketing blasts. Every message should read like it came from a real person, because it should.

The Competitive Edge Email

One of the most effective emails in the entire sequence is what I call the competitive edge email.

Most families are comparing your facility to two or three others nearby. They know it. You know it. So address it directly.

The email says something like: Susan, we know you are probably looking at a few facilities in the Tampa area. That is exactly what you should be doing. Here is what we think sets us apart. And here is an honest look at where our competitors do well too.

Then you lay out your strengths. Your staff-to-resident ratio. Your specialized care. Your review rating. Your pricing transparency.

But here is the key. You also acknowledge what your competitors do well. That is what makes this email so powerful. It is the opposite of what every other facility does.

A family reading that email thinks: If they are this straightforward and confident in an email, imagine how they treat residents. That is the kind of trust that fills beds.

This works because it addresses the comparison process head-on instead of pretending it does not exist. Every family is comparing. The facility that acknowledges that reality and positions itself honestly wins.

Offers And Incentives That Move People

Your nurturing sequence should include strategic offers at specific points. Not discounts for the sake of discounting, but incentives that move families from thinking about it to walking through your door.

The most effective offers in this space are tour-based. Come for a tour and receive a complimentary lunch with our residents. Schedule a tour this week and meet our Executive Director one on one. Book a respite stay and experience the facility firsthand with no long-term commitment.

Respite stays are particularly powerful. A family that is unsure about a permanent placement can try a two-week stay. Once the resident is settled, eating well, socializing, and comfortable, the conversation shifts from should we do this to how do we make this permanent.

Space these offers throughout the sequence. An immediate tour invitation in the first email. A respite stay offer around email eight. A limited-availability prompt around email 15. Each one gives the family a reason to act now rather than later.

Chatbots And Live Response

Adding a chatbot to your website can capture leads that would otherwise leave without making contact. Families often have pricing questions they want answered before they are willing to pick up the phone.

A simple chatbot that can answer basic questions about pricing, care types, and availability keeps visitors engaged while you or your team respond. The goal is to capture their email or phone number so your follow-up system can take over.

For smaller facilities that do not have someone available to answer calls instantly, AI-powered phone systems can handle initial inquiries. The caller gets a warm, knowledgeable response within seconds. The lead is captured and routed to your team for follow-up.

Speed wins every time in this industry. If you cannot pick up the phone within five minutes, you need a system that can.

Why This Drops Your Lead Cost By $300

The industry average lead cost is $431. Our clients consistently operate under $100. The math is simple.

When your follow-up system converts leads that would otherwise go cold, you are getting more move-ins from the same number of leads. Your cost per lead stays the same, but your cost per move-in drops dramatically.

A facility spending $3,000 per month on ads generating 30 leads has a $100 cost per lead. If their conversion rate is 5 percent because their follow-up is weak, that is 1.5 move-ins at $2,000 per move-in.

The same facility with a strong follow-up system converting at 15 percent gets 4.5 move-ins from the same 30 leads. Same ad spend. Same lead cost. But the cost per move-in drops to $667.

That is the difference between a marketing system that bleeds money and one that prints it. The follow-up system is the multiplier that makes every other channel more profitable.

Chapter 10: Reputation Management And Reviews

If you are only going to read one chapter in this book, make it this one.

I see it every single week. Facilities spending thousands on ads and thousands on referral fees with a 3.4-star rating on Google and two unanswered negative reviews sitting at the top of the page.

Every dollar they spend on marketing is wasted because families see those reviews and they are gone.

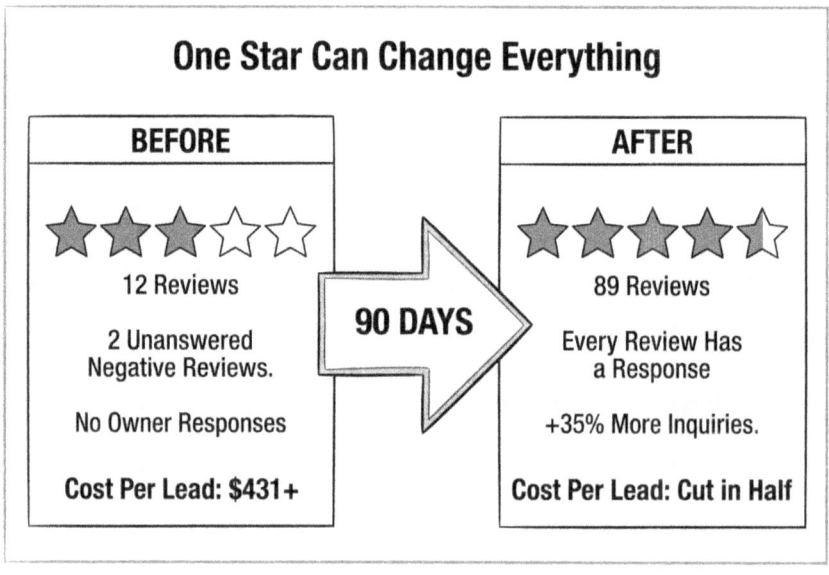

Figure 10.1: Reputation Transformation

KEY STAT: 90% of families read reviews before they call

> a facility. A one-star improvement on Google can increase your inquiry volume by 25% to 35%. For a 50-bed facility, that could mean three to five additional move-ins per year.

Your Review Scorecard

Before you do anything else, I want you to open Google right now. Look up your facility. Write down your star rating and your review count.

Then do the same on A Place for Mom, Caring.com, Facebook, and Yelp.

This takes 10 minutes and it will be the most important 10 minutes you spend this week.

Then do the same for your top five competitors. Compare the numbers side by side. If your competitor has a 4.7 with 90 reviews and you have a 3.9 with 14, you now know exactly why they are getting more tours than you.

How To Get More Reviews

Most facilities do not ask for reviews. They wait and hope. That is not a strategy.

Who To Ask

Adult children who have expressed gratitude in the last 30 days. Families who have been with you for 60 or more days and are past the adjustment period. Anyone who has mentioned a specific positive experience with a staff member, an event, or a care situation.

When To Ask

Right after someone says thank you. Right after a care review where the family is happy. Right after a community event when the emotion is fresh.

You just need to direct that positive energy toward a review.

The Ask Script

Here is what I recommend you say, word for word.

Mrs. Johnson, I just wanted to say how much we appreciate your family. I can see how much your dad has settled in and it makes our team's day when we see him smiling at breakfast. If you have had a positive experience, would you mind leaving us a quick Google review? It honestly makes a huge difference to other families who are going through what you went through when you were searching for the right place. I can text you the link right now if that is easier.

Notice what that script does. It is not pushy. It does not ask for a five-star review. It frames the request as helping other families, which appeals to the natural desire to be helpful.

Have a QR code ready on your phone that links directly to your Google review page. When someone says yes, show them the code. Make it effortless.

The Email And Text Template

For families who are not on-site, send this.

Subject: A quick favor from your facility name. Body: Hi family name. We love having resident name as part of our community and your family has been wonderful to work with. If you have two minutes, would you mind leaving us a quick Google review? It helps other families find us when they are going through the same search you went through. Here is the direct link. No pressure at all. We just appreciate you being part of our family.

Copy, paste, change the names, send. That is it.

Responding To Positive Reviews

Most facilities either do not respond to positive reviews or they paste the same generic thank you on every single one. That is a missed opportunity.

When you respond to a positive review, mention the specific staff member if one was named. That does two things. It makes the reviewer feel heard and it shows future families reading the reviews that care at your facility is personalized, not corporate.

Responding To Negative Reviews

This is where the real money is. Not because negative reviews make you money. But because how you handle a negative review tells prospective families everything they need to know about your facility.

Every negative review exists because you failed to meet someone's expectations. That is the psychology behind it. Frustration comes from the gap between what someone expected and what they experienced.

The Five-Step Response Framework

Step one. Acknowledge. Thank them for the feedback. Do not dismiss their experience.

Step two. Empathize. Show that you understand why they are upset. Validate the emotion without being defensive.

Step three. Take it offline. Provide a direct contact name and phone number to resolve the issue privately.

Step four. Protect HIPAA compliance. Never confirm or deny that someone is or was a resident. You cannot say: We are sorry about your mother's experience at our facility. That confirms residency and that is a HIPAA violation.

Step five. Follow up. After resolving the issue offline, ask if they would be willing to update their review.

> **KEY STAT: HIPAA fines for review response violations start** at $100 and go up to $50,000. Never confirm or deny that someone is or was a resident in any public response.

Turning One-Star Reviews Into Five Stars

This is something we see consistently. When you respond to a negative review with genuine accountability and a clear plan to fix the problem, reviewers often update their rating.

The jump from one star to five stars happens more frequently than one to three or one to four. When someone feels truly heard and sees real change, they do not just bump you up a point. They flip entirely.

The key is to never get defensive. Own the mistake. Explain what you are doing to fix it. Invite them back to verify. Then follow up.

Pushing Down Negative Listings In Google

Here is something most facility owners do not know about.

You might have a great 4.7-star rating on Google. But if your A Place for Mom listing has 3.1 stars from two years ago and it is sitting on page one when someone searches your facility name, families see that before they ever call you.

You cannot delete that listing. You cannot force them to change your rating. But you can push it down in the search results.

Here is how. Create fully optimized profiles on other platforms. Build backlinks to those profiles. Get reviews on those profiles. Over time, those profiles gain enough authority to outrank the negative listing.

We have pushed negative listings from position three or four down to position seven or lower. At that point, almost no one sees them.

The AI Complication

There is a new challenge that is changing how reputation management works. AI tools like Google's AI Overview, ChatGPT, and Perplexity do not just show a list of links. They read everything, including pages two, three, and beyond, and they summarize it.

So even if you push a bad listing to page five of Google, an AI tool might still pull that information into its summary and present it to a family who asks about your facility.

This is an emerging problem that requires specialized knowledge. If AI summaries are presenting negative information about your facility to families, that is not something you can fix with a template. It requires working with someone who understands how these systems source and weigh data.

Spotting And Removing Fake Reviews

Fake reviews happen in this industry more than people think. It is easier for a competitor to stack negative reviews on your profile than it is to invest in their own marketing.

Here is how to spot them. The reviewer has no other reviews on their account. The details do not match your facility, like mentioning services you do not offer. Multiple negative reviews appear within a short window, especially if a new competitor recently opened nearby. The reviewer's name does not match anyone in your system.

To get fake reviews removed, flag them in Google with a specific violation category. Gather evidence. Use the Google Business Profile Support Portal and escalate if needed.

If the reviews are clearly defamatory and you have proof they are fake, have your attorney send a cease and desist. Then contact Google and inform them that legal action is pending. In our experience, that accelerates removal significantly.

The Weekly Review Habit

The final piece is making this a habit, not a one-time project.

Fifteen minutes every Monday morning. Check Google. Check Facebook. Check the major directories. Respond to any unanswered reviews. Update your scorecard.

Set up a Google Alert for your facility name. Go to google.com/alerts, enter your business name, and set the frequency to daily. If anyone mentions your facility anywhere that Google indexes, you will get an email notification.

This is especially important for crisis management. If something negative appears online, you want to know about it the same day, not three weeks later when a family asks you about it on a tour.

The Monthly Review Generation Target

Your target is one new Google review every single week.

Here is why that is achievable. One resident typically has three to five family members who visit regularly. Each of those family members is a potential reviewer. So one resident alone could generate three to five reviews over the course of a year.

Multiply that across your facility. A 30-bed facility with an average of four engaged family members per resident has 120 potential reviewers. Getting one review per week from that pool is not aggressive. It is realistic.

The facilities that build this habit steadily pull away from their competitors. A year from now, you could have 50 more reviews than you do today. That changes everything about how families perceive you online.

FREE RESOURCE

Download the Review Scorecard, Competitor Comparison Tool, Response Templates, and Monthly Generation Calendar at seniorlivingmastery.com/senior-living-marketing-plan.

BOOK A CALL

If AI summaries or negative listings are hurting your facility, book a free call. We are the only agency in this space working on AI reputation management. seniorlivingmastery.com/book-a-call

Chapter 11: Referral Networks Everyone Ignores

Thirty-one percent of families follow their physician's recommendation when choosing a facility. Thirty-seven percent rely on recommendations from family and friends. Hospital discharge planners can generate 50 to 200 referrals per month per hospital.

These are warm, pre-qualified leads that cost you nothing.

Most facilities have never reached out to a single one of these people. They are spending thousands on Google Ads and Facebook while ignoring the highest-converting, lowest-cost lead source in the entire industry.

Referral leads convert at two to three times the rate of a paid ad. And the cost is zero.

Figure 11.1: The Referral Network Map

Hospital Discharge Planners

This is your highest-volume referral source. One relationship with one hospital discharge planner can produce five to 20 referrals per month.

Here is how it works. When a senior is hospitalized for a fall, stroke, hip fracture, or acute event, the hospital cannot discharge them until they have a safe placement. Discharge planners maintain a list of facilities they trust. If you are on that list, you get calls. If you are not, you do not exist to them.

Hospitals are also penalized financially for 30-day readmissions under Medicare's Hospital Readmissions Reduction Program. They need to move patients out safely and quickly. That urgency works in your favor.

Finding them is simple. Google the hospitals near your facility. Call the main line and ask for the discharge planning department or care transitions team. Ask for the supervisor's name and direct contact. In large hospitals, there may be five to 10 case managers handling geriatric discharges. The person you want is the director or lead case manager who sets the policy on which facilities make their preferred list.

How To Win Them Over

Do not walk in with a sales pitch. Walk in with proof.

Show them your response times. Show them your facility is immaculate. Show them your testimonials and video walkthroughs. Show them that if they send families to you, those families will be happy and their patients will be safe.

Make their job easier. Offer to pick up patients from the hospital. Handle the paperwork quickly. Be the facility that never creates problems for the discharge team.

Send a personalized email introducing your facility, your director, your care types, and your availability. Follow up with a phone call three to five days later. Then invite them to tour your facility and have lunch with your residents.

Geriatric Care Managers

Also known as aging life care professionals, these are hired by families for $150 to $250 per hour to find the right facility. When a geriatric care manager recommends your facility, that referral is gold because the family is literally paying for that professional opinion.

You can find them through aginglifecare.org.

The approach here is different from hospitals. These professionals are not trying to move patients out quickly. They are conducting thorough evaluations and their reputation depends on making the right recommendation.

Invite them in. Take them to lunch. Give them an open-door policy to visit anytime, announced or unannounced. Tell them: If we are not up to your standards, tell us where we can improve. But if you find our facility to be one of the best in the area, we would love to be on your referral list.

Elder Law Attorneys

When a family is doing Medicaid planning, estate planning, or guardianship, the attorney is often asked: Do you know a good facility?

These families are far along in the decision-making process. They are already spending money on legal help. A referral from their attorney carries enormous weight.

What makes you incredibly valuable to elder law attorneys is if you accept Medicaid and can answer Medicaid questions confidently. Most facilities cannot. If you can explain the spend-down process and what Medicaid covers in your state, attorneys will trust you and refer to you consistently.

Home Health Agencies

Home health aides visit seniors in their homes every day. They see the falls. They see missed medications. They see the weight loss. They are often the first to recognize that home care is no longer enough.

When that moment comes, the family asks the home health agency: What do we do now?

Position this as a two-way partnership. When families contact you who are not ready for assisted living, refer them to your home health partner. Reciprocity builds lasting relationships. When the time comes for assisted living, your name is the first one they mention.

Primary Care Physicians

Doctors are the hardest referral source to reach. They are busy, skeptical of sales pitches, and have pharmaceutical reps fighting for their attention all day.

Do not approach the doctor directly. Approach the practice manager. That is the person who controls what material sits in the waiting room and who gets the doctor's time.

The best way in is through educational content. Put together a booklet or scorecard that the practice can hand to families. Something like: Is It Time to Consider Assisted Living? A 10-Question Assessment. If the family scores above a certain threshold, the booklet recommends exploring options and includes your facility's information.

That approach is useful to the doctor's practice. It helps their patients. And it puts your name in front of every family going through this decision.

Other High-Value Referral Sources

Senior centers and area agencies on aging are government-funded organizations that interact with pre-assisted-living families every day. Every region in the US has one, funded under the Older Americans Act. Contact their information and referral department. Ask to be added to their provider database. Offer to present a free educational workshop with no sales pitch.

Faith communities are often the first place families turn when dealing with a parent in decline. Before they search Google, they call their pastor. Offer to host the senior group at your facility for a tour, lunch, and fellowship.

Financial advisors and long-term care insurance agents work with higher-income, privately-paid families. When the insurance policy gets activated, the advisor is asked where the parent should go. If you accept LTC insurance, detail which carriers you work with and build relationships with local agents.

Rehabilitation centers and skilled nursing facilities discharge patients who cannot safely go home after a hip fracture or stroke. The rehab facility's social worker refers them to assisted living. Same approach as hospitals: find the social worker, build the relationship.

Government agencies including Adult Protective Services, Veterans Affairs, Medicaid waiver programs, and the 211 helpline all interact with vulnerable seniors and their families. If you accept VA Aid and Attendance benefits, contact your regional VA medical center's social work department.

The Facility One-Pager

Before you start any outreach, create a one-pager. This is a single printed page that sits on the discharge planner's desk, in the attorney's file, and on the doctor's referral bulletin board.

It should include your facility name and address prominently, your director and admissions contact with a direct phone number, care types, bed count, current availability, starting monthly rates, your top three to four differentiators in brief phrases, one real facility photo, your state license number, any awards, and QR codes linking to a virtual tour and your website.

Print a hundred of these. Have them ready for every meeting.

The 90-Day Referral Building System

Weeks one and two. Build your prospect list. Work through all 12 referral categories. Google each type plus your city. Fill in prospect names and contacts. Your goal is 60 to 120 names.

Weeks three through six. First outreach. Send 10 to 15 personalized emails per week. Follow up every email with a phone call three to five days later. Schedule drop-off visits to hospitals and physician practices.

Weeks seven through 10. Deepen relationships. Host your first luncheon at your facility. Invite every contact who responded positively. Give them a full tour. Feed them. Let them meet residents and staff. Send a thank-you note after every visit.

Weeks 11 and 12. Systematize and maintain. Send monthly email updates to all referral partners with your current availability. Schedule quarterly in-person visits with your top 10 partners. Track every referral in your CRM.

The ongoing maintenance takes less than an hour per month. Send the availability update. Reprint the one-pagers. Send thank-you notes. Schedule visits. Invite one new partner for a tour. Review your tracking.

Facilities that do outreach once and disappear get nothing. Facilities that show up consistently every month build referral pipelines that produce residents for years.

> **KEY STAT: Referral leads convert at 2 to 3 times the rate** of paid advertising leads. One hospital discharge planner relationship can produce 5 to 20 referrals per month at zero cost.

Chapter 12: Converting Tours And Your 90-Day Action Plan

The industry average tour-to-move-in rate is 20 to 35 percent. That means most families who took the time to drive to your facility, walk through, ask questions, and meet your team still chose someone else.

Here is the math. Say you get 10 tours per month. At a 25 percent conversion rate, that is 2.5 move-ins. Improve that to 35 percent and you get 3.5 move-ins. That one extra move-in per month, over a year, represents over $124,000 in additional lifetime revenue.

Sixty-three percent of families say the feeling they got during a tour was the single biggest factor in their decision. Not the price. Not the amenities. The feeling.

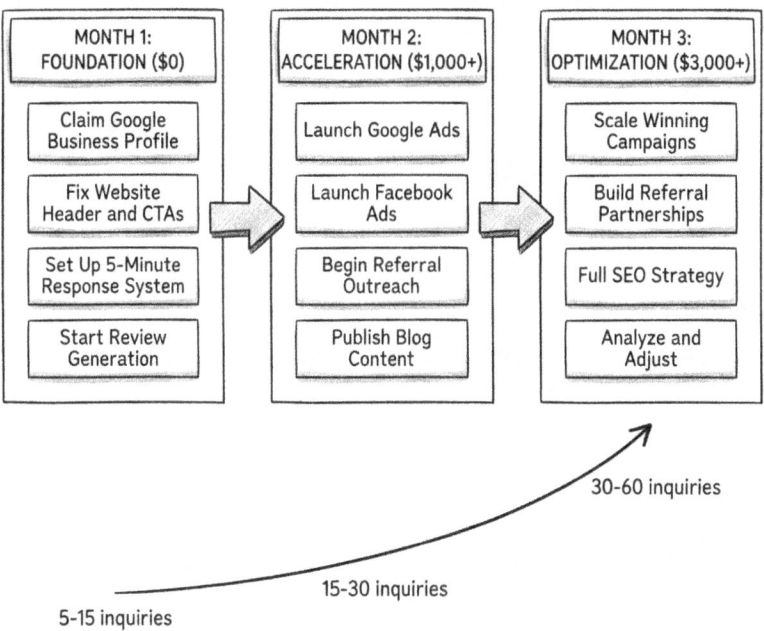

Figure 12.1: The 90-Day Marketing Roadmap

Know Your Buyer

Most facilities treat every family the same way. Same tour. Same pitch. Same follow-up. That is why they convert at 25 percent.

There are four distinct buyer personas that cover virtually every family who tours your facility.

The Overwhelmed Daughter

This is 60 to 70 percent of all your tours. An adult daughter, age 45 to 65, who works full-time and has kids of her own. She has been managing her parent's care for months or years. There was a fall, a hospital stay, or she simply cannot do it anymore.

Her emotional state is guilt, exhaustion, and fear. She is terrified she is abandoning her mother.

How you sell to her: empathy first. Acknowledge the guilt before you show her a single room. Say: I know this is incredibly hard. I want you to know that you are doing the right thing. Researching, touring, asking questions. This is not giving up on your mom. This is fighting for her.

Let her take her time. Do not rush the tour. Introduce her to current family members who went through a similar experience. When you show her the room, say: Can you picture mom here? Then stop talking.

The Crisis Placer

Fifteen to 20 percent of tours. The hospital called. Mom cannot go home. They need a bed by Friday.

Be the calm in the storm. Have answers immediately. Walk them through the admission process step by step. Show them you can move fast without cutting corners.

The Planner

Ten to 15 percent. No crisis. Planning ahead. Analytical. They will take six to 12 months and they want data.

Give them the pricing sheet. The state inspection records. Care level transition details. Do not pressure them. Give them a reason to put down a refundable deposit to hold a room.

The Reluctant Spouse

Five to 10 percent. A husband whose wife has dementia and he can no longer care for her at home. He feels like he is giving up.

Honor his grief. Do not diminish what he has done as a caregiver. Position the move as: You are getting your wife a team so you can go back to being her husband.

Pre-Tour Preparation

Everything that matters during a tour starts 24 hours before the family arrives.

When you confirm the tour, do not just say see you tomorrow. Say: We are looking forward to meeting you. Is there anything specific you would like to see or any questions on your mind? Send directions, parking information, and what to expect.

Review the persona notes from the booking call. If they mentioned mom loves gardening, you now know where to start the tour.

Stage the best available room. Fresh linens, lights on, flowers if possible. It has to smell fantastic.

Brief your staff. The Johnson family is touring at 2pm. The resident is their mother Margaret. She loves birds and used to teach piano. Every staff member should be ready to greet the family warmly by name.

Time the tour during active hours. The family needs to see residents eating, socializing, playing cards, and doing activities. Not sleeping in front of a television.

Have the specific room pricing printed and ready. If the family asks how much this costs and you say I will have to get back to you on that, you have already lost them.

During The Tour

Greet the family by name at the door. Not from behind a desk. At the door.

Ask an open question immediately: Before we start, tell me about your mom. What is she like? This shifts the entire dynamic from transactional to personal.

Personalize the tour path. If mom loves gardening, start in the courtyard. If dad was in the military, introduce him to residents who served.

Introduce staff by name and story. This is Maria. She has been with us for six years. She makes the best coffee on the floor. Staff who have names and stories feel like family, not employees.

Walk through the dining room near mealtime. Let them smell the food. Let them see it. Offer them lunch.

End at the best available room. Walk them in. Let them look around. Say: This is the room that would be available for your mom. It gets morning light. It is close to the dining room and the garden.

Then ask: Can you picture mom here? Stop talking. Let the silence do the work. If they start mentally placing furniture, you are closing.

What To Avoid

Talking too much. Families remember feelings, not monologues. Being too clinical. Speak in plain language, not medical jargon. Rushing. Budget 60 to 90 minutes. If they want to stay longer, let them.

And this is crucial. When they ask how much it costs, answer directly with a specific number. For this room, at your mom's care level, the monthly rate would be a specific dollar amount. That includes meals, housekeeping, personal care, activities, and medication management.

Never dodge the cost question.

Post-Tour Follow-Up

The tour is not the end of the sale. It is the middle.

Same day, within two hours. Call them. Hi Sarah, it is Maria from your facility. I just wanted to thank you for coming in today. How was the drive home? How are you feeling about everything?

Then send an email. A personalized recap, not a template. Reference something specific from the tour. Attach a photo of the room they saw. Include the pricing sheet and clear next steps.

Day three. Text or call. Any questions since the tour? Happy to answer anything, even the hard ones. If siblings could not attend, offer to schedule a second tour.

Day seven. Send a family testimonial from a family with a similar situation.

Day 14. Direct but caring. I have been thinking about your family. How is the search going? If they are stalling, provide legitimate availability context. The room I showed you is still available, but two other families toured it this week.

Do not stop until they move in, choose another facility, or explicitly tell you to stop. Not ready yet is not no. It means I am scared and I need more time.

The 100-Objection Playbook

In the downloadable playbook, there are 100 specific objections that families raise during the sales process, organized into 10 categories. For each objection, the playbook includes what the family really means behind the words and a word-for-word response.

Cost and financial concerns. Fifteen objections covering everything from it is too expensive to what if the money runs out.

Timing and readiness. Ten objections. We are not ready yet. We need to think about it. Mom is doing fine right now.

Parent resistance. Fifteen objections and the most emotional category. Mom says she does not want to go. She says she would rather die than move into a home. My siblings think she should stay at home.

Quality of care, facility comparisons, logistics, guilt and emotional concerns, trust and credibility, specific care situations, and final decisions round out the remaining categories.

Print this section. Keep it at the admissions desk. Role-play these with your team weekly. The facilities that handle objections confidently and with empathy are the ones converting at 35 to 40 percent.

> **KEY STAT: 63% of families say the feeling they got during** a tour was the single biggest factor in their decision. Personalizing the experience to each buyer persona is what separates 25% conversion rates from 35% and above.

Your 90-Day Marketing Action Plan

This is where everything in this book comes together. Not new strategies. The same strategies you have already learned, organized into a week-by-week execution plan.

Because you can know everything about Google Ads, SEO, reviews, referrals, and follow-up systems. But if you do not know what you are doing on Monday morning, none of it matters.

Budget Tiers

Zero dollars. Everything in month one is free. You can build a working marketing system on nothing. It is slower, but it works. At this tier, expect five to 15 new inquiries per month by day 90.

One thousand dollars per month. This gets you into Google Ads and basic Facebook targeting on top of the organic work. Expect 15 to 30 inquiries per month by day 90.

Three thousand dollars per month. Fully paid system across Google, Facebook, and Bing plus everything else. Expect 30 to 60 or more inquiries per month, with four to eight additional move-ins.

Every task in the plan is tagged by budget tier. If it says all, everyone does it regardless of budget. If it says 1K plus, it only applies if you are spending at least a thousand per month.

Month One: The Foundation

You are not launching ads in month one. You are not writing a blog. You are auditing everything, fixing what is broken, and building the infrastructure so that when you start driving traffic, it actually converts.

Week one. Audit and assess. Complete your Google Business Profile with every field filled and 20 or more real photos uploaded. Run through the website audit: phone number visible, call-to-action above the fold, real photos, load speed, pricing visible, testimonials on the homepage. Identify your top five competitors and compare your ratings against theirs across all platforms. Set up your lead tracker.

Week two. Fix what is broken. Address your top three website issues from the audit. Respond to every unanswered review on all platforms. Create your direct Google review link. Claim and complete your profiles on all major directories.

Week three. Start generating reviews and publishing content. Your goal is five new Google reviews in month one using the scripts from Chapter 10. Publish your first two blog posts using the AI content system from Chapter 6. Train your front desk on five-minute response times.

Week four. Build your referral prospect list using the system from Chapter 11. Review your month one progress.

Month Two: Launch

Week five. If you have budget, this is where Google Ads and Facebook Ads go live. Campaign structure, keyword selection, location targeting, and landing page setup are all covered in Chapter 8. If you have no ad budget, push harder on organic content, Google Business Profile posts, and review generation.

Week six. Begin referral outreach. Ten to 15 personalized emails per week to your prospect list. Follow up with phone calls. Schedule facility tours for your referral contacts. Build out your lead follow-up system from Chapter 9.

Week seven. First real look at your ad data. What is your cost per lead? What is your click-through rate? Cut what is not working. Scale what is.

Week eight. Month two review. Total leads by source, average response time, tours booked, move-ins, cost per lead, Google reviews gained, and website traffic. Compare everything to month one.

Month Three: Scale And Optimize

Week nine. Optimize paid channels. Top-performing keywords get more budget. Underperformers get paused.

Week 10. Review your tour-to-move-in conversion rate using the systems earlier in this chapter. Mystery shop your own facility. Have someone call pretending to be a family looking for placement. See how your team handles it. How fast they respond. How the conversation goes. It will be eye-opening.

Week 11. Reputation and content expansion. Continue the monthly review generation system. Expand your blog content. Deepen referral partner relationships.

Week 12. Fill in the 90-day tracker. Day one baseline compared to day 90. Star rating, review count, leads, response time, tours, move-ins, cost per lead, cost per move-in. Set targets for the next quarter and keep going.

10 Mistakes That Kill This Plan

One. Skipping month one and jumping straight into ads. If your Google Business Profile is not done, your website does not convert, and your team does not respond to leads quickly, you are paying to send families to a bad experience.

Two. Slow lead response. If I sound like a broken record, good. This is the biggest revenue leak in senior living. Every other marketing activity in this plan is worthless if your team takes 12 to 48 hours to call someone back.

Three. Giving up on ads after two weeks. Google Ads needs at least 30 days of optimization. Two months is the minimum I set with every client before evaluating performance.

Four. Asking for reviews once and then stopping. This is a monthly habit. Five to 10 requests per month, every month.

Five. Not tracking anything. If you cannot tell me your cost per lead and cost per move-in by source, you are guessing. Guessing is expensive.

Six. Building a referral list and never following up. One email is not a relationship. Consistency over months is what builds a referral pipeline.

Seven. Ignoring your online reputation while running ads. Every dollar you spend on advertising is wasted if families see a 3.2-star rating.

Eight. Running the same tour for every family. Know your buyer personas. Personalize the experience.

Nine. Not briefing your staff before tours. The family should feel expected and welcomed, not like they are interrupting someone's day.

Ten. Trying to do everything at once. Follow the week-by-week plan. Build the foundation first. Then layer on paid, referrals, and advanced strategies.

FREE RESOURCE

Download the complete 90-Day Marketing Action Plan, the 100-Objection Playbook, and all tracking templates at seniorlivingmastery.com/senior-living-marketing-plan.

Chapter 13: AI And The Future Of Senior Living Marketing

Everything I have covered in this book works today. It has been tested across hundreds of facilities and it produces results.

But the landscape is shifting. Artificial intelligence is changing how families find information, how they evaluate facilities, and how they make decisions. If you are not paying attention to this, you will be caught off guard.

I am not talking about some distant future. This is happening right now. And it will accelerate.

How Families Will Find You In Two Years

Right now, most families start their search on Google. They type in assisted living plus their city, look at the results, click a few links, read some reviews, and start making calls.

That process is already changing. Google's AI Overview now appears at the top of many search results. Instead of showing ten blue links, Google reads multiple websites, synthesizes the information, and presents a summary directly in the search results.

A daughter searching for the best assisted living in Fort Lauderdale might never click a single link. She reads the AI summary, which pulls information from your website, your reviews, your directory listings, and your competitors' content, and makes her decision based on what the AI presents.

ChatGPT, Perplexity, and other AI assistants are doing the same thing. Families are starting to ask AI tools directly: What are the best assisted living facilities near me? What should I look for in a memory care facility? How much does assisted living cost in my area?

These tools do not show a list of links. They read everything available online, including pages two, three, and beyond in Google, and they summarize it in a conversational answer. The facility with the strongest, most comprehensive online presence gets mentioned. The facility with thin content and bad reviews gets left out.

What This Means For Your SEO

Traditional SEO is not dying. But it is evolving. The strategies in Chapters 4 through 7 of this book are still the foundation. You still need a fast, well-structured website. You still need quality content. You still need backlinks and a strong Google Business Profile.

What changes is that the bar for content quality goes up. AI tools prioritize websites that provide detailed, authoritative, well-organized information. Thin pages with 200 words of generic content will not get picked up by AI summaries. Comprehensive pages that answer real questions in depth will.

This is why the topical authority strategy from Chapter 6 matters more than ever. The facility with 30 in-depth blog posts covering every aspect of senior living in their local market is the one that AI tools reference. The facility with a five-page website is invisible to them.

What This Means For Your Reputation

This is where it gets serious.

In Chapter 10, I explained how to push down negative listings in Google by building optimized profiles on other platforms. That strategy still works for traditional search results.

But AI tools do not just read page one. They read everything. Pages two, three, five, ten. If there is a negative review of your facility buried on page five of Google that no human would ever find, an AI tool might still pull it into its summary and present it to a family.

That changes the game completely. You can no longer rely on suppression alone. You need to ensure that the overall volume of positive, accurate information about your facility far outweighs any negative content anywhere online.

This means generating more reviews consistently, publishing more content, building more directory profiles, and actively managing your online presence across every platform. The facilities that treat reputation as a monthly habit rather than a one-time project will be the ones that AI tools present favorably.

AI Tools You Can Use Today

AI is not just a threat to prepare for. It is a tool you can use right now to gain an advantage over competitors who are not paying attention.

Content creation. The AI content system I described in Chapter 6 uses tools like ChatGPT and Google Gemini to research topics, generate outlines, and draft blog posts. You still need to edit and personalize the output, but AI cuts the content creation time by 70 to 80 percent.

Lead nurturing. The 90-day email system from Chapter 9 is built entirely with AI. You provide the profile document, feed it into an AI tool, and it generates a personalized 20-email sequence in minutes. That system has saved our clients hundreds of thousands of dollars in aggregate.

Ad copy and testing. AI tools can generate multiple versions of ad headlines and descriptions in seconds. Instead of writing one ad and hoping it works, you can test five variations and let the data tell you which one converts.

Chatbots and phone systems. AI-powered chatbots on your website can answer family questions instantly, 24 hours a day. AI phone systems can handle initial inquiries when your team is unavailable. These tools ensure you never miss a lead, which in this industry is the difference between filling a bed and losing one.

What AI Cannot Replace

AI is a tool, not a replacement for the human elements that actually fill beds.

It cannot replace the warmth of a real person answering the phone. It cannot replace a genuine tour where a family meets your staff and sees your residents laughing together at lunch. It cannot replace the relationship you build with a hospital discharge planner over years of consistent, reliable service.

The facilities that will win in the next five years are the ones that use AI to handle the repetitive, time-consuming tasks like content creation, email sequences, and data analysis while their human team focuses on what only humans can do. Building trust. Showing empathy. Closing the sale.

Use AI to work faster and smarter. But never lose sight of the fact that this industry is built on human connection. A daughter placing her mother in your care is making one of the most emotional decisions of her life. No AI tool will ever replace the person who looks her in the eye and says: Your mom will be safe here.

The Bottom Line

AI is not something to fear. It is something to prepare for and to use.

If you have implemented the strategies in this book, you are already ahead of 90 percent of facilities. Strong SEO, quality content, a comprehensive online presence, consistent review generation, and active reputation management are exactly what AI tools prioritize when they decide which facilities to recommend.

The facilities that ignore AI will slowly become invisible. The facilities that embrace it will have an unfair advantage.

We are actively working on AI reputation management and AI search optimization at Senior Living Mastery. If you want to stay ahead of these changes, reach out. We are the only agency in this space working on this specifically.

Conclusion: The Facilities That Win

You now have the complete system.

Not theory. Not concepts. The exact playbook that has taken facilities from near-closure to full occupancy. From bleeding money on referral agencies to generating their own leads at a fraction of the cost. From hoping the phone rings to knowing exactly where the next move-in is coming from.

Everything in this book is built from real data, real campaigns, and real results across hundreds of facilities.

But I want to be direct with you about something.

The facilities that win are not the ones with the biggest budgets. They are not the ones with the nicest buildings or the most beds. They are the ones that execute.

They optimize their Google Business Profile and keep it updated. They fix their website so it converts visitors into calls. They respond to every lead within five minutes. They ask for reviews every month. They build referral relationships and show up consistently. They run tours that are personalized to each family. They follow up until the family moves in or tells them to stop.

None of this is complicated. All of it requires consistency.

If you implement even half of what is in this book, you will see results. If you implement all of it, you will transform your facility's marketing and your occupancy.

Here is where to start. If you have not done anything yet, do these three things this week.

One. Claim and optimize your Google Business Profile. It is free and it is the highest-ROI activity in this entire book.

Two. Put your phone number on every page of your website with a click-to-call button on mobile.

Three. Respond to every lead within five minutes. That one habit will do more for your occupancy than any amount of ad spend.

If you want help implementing any of this, or if you want us to build and manage the entire system for you, book a free 30-minute discovery call at seniorlivingmastery.com. We guarantee you will walk away with actionable insights, even if we never work together.

We wrote the book on senior living marketing. Literally. You are holding it.

Now go fill some beds.

BOOK A CALL

Free 30-minute discovery call. We will review your
current marketing, identify your biggest opportunities,

and give you a clear action plan.

seniorlivingmastery.com/book-a-call

About The Author

I am an Australian entrepreneur, a former Australian Army veteran, and the founder of Senior Living Mastery. My time in the army was cut short by an injury I sustained during service. But soldiers adapt. That is what we do. I took everything the military taught me about discipline, systems, and performing under pressure, and I put it all into building businesses.

My first company was TWECS, a telecommunications business. I built it from zero to $5.7 million in annual revenue with over 30 employees. That experience taught me what it actually takes to scale a company, manage a team, and make tough calls when real money is on the line.

After TWECS, I spent years building businesses across multiple countries before establishing Senior Living Mastery out of Fort Lauderdale, Florida. Fort Lauderdale was a deliberate choice. I am a sailing fanatic, and if you know anything about South Florida, you know there is no better place to be on the water. Between the sailing, the fishing, and the energy of the city, it was the perfect base for what I wanted to build.

But the reason I ended up in the senior living space was personal.

I have always loved spending time with seniors. Growing up, some of my favorite memories were sitting with my grandparents, just listening to their stories and learning about their lives. There is something irreplaceable about those conversations. The wisdom, the humor, the perspective that only comes from decades of experience.

One of my favorite traditions from the Australian Army was Anzac Day. That is the day Australians and New Zealanders honor their military veterans. Every year, veterans from every generation come together, and the older guys share their war stories. The battles they fought, the friends they lost, the lives they built after service. I could sit and listen to those men and women for hours. It was fascinating, and it shaped how I see the world.

So when I got into digital marketing and started working with senior living facilities, I saw pretty quickly that something was broken in this industry. The big referral directories and lead generation companies were not built to help residents. They were built to squeeze money out of facility owners.

They would send garbage leads, charge thousands per placement, and the residents would often not even stay. The business model actually rewarded short stays because the faster a resident left, the faster they could place someone new and collect another fee. That is not care. That is a racket.

That is why I built Assisted Living Near Mom. I wanted to create something different. A directory with over 7,000 facilities that genuinely helps families find the right fit for their loved ones. Does it help facility owners generate leads and revenue? Absolutely. But it does it the right way. We will always put the well-being of potential residents above any payment from any facility. That is not a tagline. That is how we run things.

I am a God-fearing man, and it matters to me that we look after the people who spent their lives looking after us. Our parents. Our grandparents. Our veterans. They deserve way better than being treated like a dollar sign.

Senior Living Mastery is the only marketing agency in the country built exclusively for senior living facilities. We are a smaller team compared to the big players, and honestly, I think that is our biggest advantage. Every client works directly with us. Every strategy is custom built for their facility, their market, their goals. We do not farm the work out and we do not treat anyone like a number.

When I am not working, I am with my wife and my son. I am a huge sports guy. Growing up in Australia, cricket and rugby were everything to me. Being around American sports got me hooked on baseball too. And when I need to decompress, you will find me on the water. Sailing and deep-sea fishing are my reset button, and Fort Lauderdale is hard to beat for both.

I love this industry and I love the people in it. I wrote this book because I believe every facility owner deserves access to the same marketing playbook that the big chains run, without having to pay big chain prices for it.

If anything in this book made a difference for you, I would love to hear about it. And if you want a hand putting any of it into action, you know where to find me.

seniorlivingmastery.com/book-a-call

Resources

At Senior Living Mastery, we have built over 30 templates, tools, calculators, and guides specifically for senior living facility owners. Everything is designed to help you implement the strategies in this book without starting from scratch.

All of these resources are available for free at seniorlivingmastery.com/senior-living-marketing-plan.

Here is a look at what you will find.

Cost Per Bed Calculator. Plug in your bed count, occupancy rate, and average monthly rate. It calculates exactly how much revenue you are losing from empty beds and shows you the ROI of filling just one or two more per month.

90-Day Marketing Action Plan Template. The detailed, week-by-week execution plan from Chapter 12, formatted as a printable tracker. Every task, every deadline, every milestone laid out so you know exactly what to do and when.

Buyer Persona Builder. A fillable template for mapping out your ideal family decision-maker. Demographics, emotional profile, search behavior, objections, and messaging guidelines. The same framework we use with every client.

Local SEO Audit Template. A step-by-step checklist for auditing your Google Business Profile, website, citations, and local rankings against your top competitors.

Review Generation Scripts and Templates. Word-for-word scripts for asking families for reviews, response templates for positive and negative reviews, and the QR code setup guide from Chapter 10.

Google Ads Campaign Setup Guide. A complete, in-depth walkthrough for building your first senior living Google Ads campaign. Campaign structure, keyword selection, ad copy templates, negative keyword lists, location targeting, and bid strategy. Everything from Chapter 8 in a step-by-step format.

Facebook Ads Setup Guide. The same level of detail for Facebook. Audience targeting, creative guidelines, lead form setup, retargeting configuration, and budget allocation by tier.

Website Audit Checklist. The 7-point website fix from Chapter 3 plus the 10 essential pages checklist and the quick wins action list, all in one printable document.

Referral Partner Outreach Templates. Email scripts, phone call frameworks, and follow-up sequences for building referral relationships with hospitals, attorneys, physicians, and community organizations from Chapter 11.

Facility Management and Sales Improvement Guides. Templates for tracking tour-to-move-in conversion rates, improving your admissions process, training your front desk team on five-minute response times, and building a follow-up system.

Content Marketing Planner. A 12-month content calendar template built around the five content pillars from Chapter 6. Includes topic ideas, keyword targets, and publishing schedules.

Competitive Intelligence Tracker. A spreadsheet for monitoring your competitors across Google rankings, review counts, ad activity, and website changes.

New templates and tools are added regularly. If you have a specific challenge that is not covered, reach out. We build tools based on what facility owners actually need.

And remember, our YouTube channel has full video walkthroughs for many of these templates. Search Senior Living Mastery on YouTube for step-by-step tutorials on everything from Google Ads setup to reputation management systems.

If you want hands-on help implementing any of the strategies in this book, book a free 30-minute discovery call at seniorlivingmastery.com/book-a-call. We guarantee you walk away with actionable advice, even if we never work together.

Appendix

The following worksheets, checklists, and quick reference guides are designed to help you put the strategies in this book into action. Photocopy them, download the digital versions at seniorlivingmastery.com/senior-living-marketing-plan, or write directly in the book. These are your tools. Use them.

Marketing Audit Scorecard

Use this scorecard to audit your facility against the standards in this book. Rate each item from 1 to 10, where 1 means not started and 10 means fully optimized. Be honest. The facilities that improve the fastest are the ones that face reality head on.

Website

Phone number visible above the fold on every page _____ / 10

Clear call to action (Schedule a Tour, Call Now) above the fold _____ / 10

Real photos of your facility (not stock images) _____ / 10

Mobile responsive and easy to use on a phone _____ / 10

Pricing information visible (not hidden behind a form) _____ / 10

Testimonials or reviews embedded on the homepage _____ / 10

SSL certificate active (no security warnings) _____ / 10

Google Business Profile

Profile fully completed with all fields filled _____ / 10

50 or more real photos uploaded _____ / 10

At least one new Google review per week _____ / 10

Star rating of 4.5 or higher _____ / 10

Responding to every review (positive and negative) _____ / 10

Weekly Google Posts with photos _____ / 10

Reputation Management

Review generation system in place with QR codes _____ / 10

Staff trained on when and how to ask for reviews _____ / 10

Profiles claimed on all major directories _____ / 10

Consistent NAP information across all listings _____ / 10

Negative reviews addressed within 24 hours _____ / 10

Lead Follow-Up

Average response time under 5 minutes _____ / 10

Automated text and email follow-up system active _____ / 10

15 to 30 touchpoints built into follow-up sequence _____ / 10

Lead tracking system in place _____ / 10

No leads falling through the cracks _____ / 10

Paid Advertising

Google Ads campaign running with proper structure _____ / 10

Facebook Ads with retargeting active _____ / 10

Conversion tracking installed on all platforms _____ / 10

Cost per lead tracked and optimized monthly _____ / 10

Separate campaigns for each care type _____ / 10

Content and SEO

At least 20 blog posts published _____ / 10

Content covers all five pillars _____ / 10

Schema markup installed on website _____ / 10

Local keywords targeted in content _____ / 10

Backlink building strategy active _____ / 10

Referral Network

Active referral relationships with 10 or more partners _____ / 10
Regular outreach and follow-up with referral sources _____ / 10
Referral partners have toured your facility _____ / 10
Tracking referral source for each lead _____ / 10

Total Score: Add up all individual scores. Maximum possible is 360.

Below 120: Your marketing needs a complete overhaul. Start with Chapter 12 and the 90-day plan.

120 to 200: You have a foundation but major gaps. Prioritize the lowest-scoring categories first.

200 to 280: Solid base. Focus on optimization and scaling what is already working.

Above 280: You are in the top 10% of facilities. Fine-tune and protect your position.

Monthly Marketing Tracker

Photocopy this page or download the printable version at seniorlivingmastery.com/senior-living-marketing-plan. Fill it in at the end of every month. The facilities that track their numbers are the ones that grow.

Month: _____ **Year:** _____

Total website visitors: _____

Total phone calls received: _____

Total form submissions: _____

Total leads (all sources combined): _____

Leads from Google Ads: _____

Leads from Facebook Ads: _____

Leads from organic search: _____

Leads from referrals: _____

Leads from directories (A Place for Mom, Assisted Living Near Mom, etc.): _____

Average response time to new leads: _____

Total tours booked: _____

Total tours completed: _____

Tour to move-in conversion rate: _____

Total move-ins this month: _____

Cost per lead (total ad spend divided by total leads): _____

Cost per tour (total ad spend divided by tours booked): _____

Cost per move-in (total ad spend divided by move-ins): _____

Current occupancy rate: _____

Number of empty beds: _____

Revenue from empty beds lost (empty beds x $5,667): _____

Google review count (start of month): _____

Google review count (end of month): _____

New reviews added this month: _____

Current Google star rating: _____

Blog posts published this month: _____

Google Business Profile posts this month: _____

Referral partner meetings this month: _____

Notes and observations for the month:

_____

_____

_____

_____

_____

Quick Reference: Key Numbers

Tear this page out and pin it above your desk. These are the numbers that matter most in senior living marketing.

$68,000 Annual revenue lost per empty bed

$431 Average cost per lead in senior living

$5,000 to $7,000 Average referral agency placement fee

$3 to $5 Average cost per click on Google Ads for senior living

78% Families who trust online reviews as much as personal recommendations

73% Families who start their search with a generic Google search

5 minutes Maximum response time to convert leads at the highest rate

100x How much better a 5-minute response converts vs. a 30-minute response

70 to 100 days Average timeline from first contact to move-in

15 to 30 Number of touchpoints needed before a family commits

3 to 5 Number of facilities a family compares before deciding

65% to 70% Senior living searches that happen on mobile devices

4.3 million Monthly searches in the US for senior living related terms

10,000 Americans who turn 65 every single day

$94.2 billion Total US assisted living market value

50+ Minimum photos your Google Business Profile should have

1 per week Target for new Google reviews

52% Adult daughters aged 45 to 65 who are the primary decision makers

Quick Reference: Website Fixes

These are the fastest wins you can implement today. Each one costs nothing and takes less than an hour. Check them off as you complete them.

- ☐ Add phone number to every page with click-to-call on mobile
- ☐ Add a Schedule a Tour button above the fold on every page
- ☐ Replace all stock photos with real photos of your facility
- ☐ Add pricing information to your website (do not hide it)
- ☐ Embed Google reviews on your homepage
- ☐ Add a video walkthrough of your facility
- ☐ Make sure your site loads in under 3 seconds on mobile
- ☐ Update the copyright year in your footer
- ☐ Add SSL certificate if you do not have one
- ☐ Remove any autoplay music or video
- ☐ Add schema markup for local business
- ☐ Create separate pages for each care type you offer
- ☐ Add an FAQ page with common family questions
- ☐ Put your content on pages, not in downloadable PDFs
- ☐ Add a dedicated Schedule a Tour page (separate from Contact)
- ☐ Add staff photos and bios to your About page
- ☐ Add a What to Expect or Move-In Guide page
- ☐ Test your entire website on a mobile phone and fix anything broken

Quick Reference: Google Business Profile Setup

Your Google Business Profile is the single highest-ROI activity in this entire book. Use this checklist to make sure yours is fully optimized.

- [ ] Claim and verify your Google Business Profile
- [ ] Business name matches your facility exactly (no keyword stuffing)
- [ ] Primary category set to Assisted Living Facility
- [ ] Add all relevant secondary categories
- [ ] Full business description written with services and location mentioned
- [ ] Phone number matches your website exactly
- [ ] Address matches your website and all directory listings exactly
- [ ] Website URL set to your homepage
- [ ] Hours set to 24/7 (you are a residential facility)
- [ ] Upload 50 or more real photos of your facility
- [ ] Add exterior photos (5 to 10 minimum)
- [ ] Add interior and common area photos
- [ ] Add resident room photos (at least 5)
- [ ] Add staff interacting with residents photos
- [ ] Add outdoor space and garden photos
- [ ] Create your Google review link
- [ ] Generate a QR code from your review link
- [ ] Print QR code and place at front desk and common areas
- [ ] Respond to every existing review (positive and negative)
- [ ] Set up weekly Google Posts with photos and Call Now button

- ☐ Add services and amenities to your profile
- ☐ Add your service area
- ☐ Enable messaging if available

Notes

Notes

Notes

Notes

Notes

Notes

Notes

Notes

Notes

Notes

Notes

Notes

Our Marketing Comes With Guarantees

seniorlivingmastery.com/book-a-call

If you are a senior living facility and you want help and advice, our work always comes with a guarantee. That means even if you do not end up working with us, we still guarantee you walk away with valuable and actionable advice. Book a free call today.

www.ingramcontent.com/pod-product-compliance
Lightning Source LLC
Chambersburg PA
CBHW071030240526
45469CB00006BD/2160